DAILY WORD

Daily readings from The Word, with commentary and prayers by Reg Lang

Edited by Cornelis PJ Visser-Marchant

Original edition (1962) published by:
The Missionary Society of the New Church, London
This edition (2025) published by:
Freedom Philosophy

Some rights reserved. No part of this publication may be produced, distributed, or transmitted in any form for commercial purposes without written permission from the publisher.

For bulk orders please contact the editor:
Telephone/SMS: +61 416243242
All purchases available via online retailers
Printed in Australia

Publisher's Cataloging-in-Publication data
Lang, Reg; Visser-Marchant, Cornelis PJ
Daily Readings from the Word
Religion & Spirituality / Cor Visser-Marchant
400p. 10x15cm
ISBN 978-0645074321 (paperback)
1. Religion - Spirituality - Spiritual Philosophy
Edited Print: Second Edition

DAILY READINGS FROM THE WORD

With commentary and prayers by Reg Lang

Edited by Cor Visser-Marchant

"It is written, Man shall not live by bread alone, but by every word that proceeds out of the mouth of God."

MATTHEW 4:4

The Lord's Prayer

Our Father in the heavens,
hallowed be your name.
Your kingdom come.
Your will be done, as in heaven,
so upon the earth.
Give us today our daily bread.
And forgive us our debts,
as we also forgive our debtors.
And do not lead us into temptation,
but deliver us from evil.
For yours is the kingdom
and the power
and the glory, for ever.
Amen

Daily Word

Editor's Introduction

This edited version was prepared as a tribute to the original work (1962) by Reg Lang, which is now no longer available in print.

Drawing from the Bible and revelations of Emanuel Swedenborg, you will discover the forgotten ancient sacred wisdom that holds the key to opening our eyes to The Word for personal spiritual insight, which will also strengthen your faith and personal connection with the Divine: our Lord Jesus Christ! This work is therefore of considerable value (like the 'Pearl of Great Price') to everyone seeking to draw from everlasting well of truth and our Lord Jesus Christ: The Living Word.

To this end the editor has taken the liberty to recreate and update this marvelous book to ensure it is made available once more and able to be properly catalogued and preserved for future generations.

A few minor changes have been made for this edition: some of the formatting change was needed to make publication easier, some of the older language has been updated to be a little more contemporary and easier to read for the modern mind and those less familiar with English, and the appendix of references has been omitted.

Also added are a couple of brief chapters that may help introduce the reader to study the scriptures more spiritually.

Below follows the original foreword from the author: Reginald Lang.
Cor

Foreword

IN THE "Daily Readings" the plan followed has been a simple one designed to achieve the best results. Its purpose is to provide a Subject for Meditation from The Word, in the form of a quotation. This has been followed by a Commentary which seeks to bring out clearly the inner spiritual lesson. Finally, a Prayer is offered, inspired from various portions of The Word.

An Appendix at the end of this little book supplies the particular reference to the Prayer for each day, although the wording has, in some cases, been adapted to the prayer form.

It should be emphasized that this is a publication of the New Church and, as such, the lessons brought out in the Commentary for each day are entirely drawn from the Heavenly Doctrines revealed by the Lord through His servant Emanuel Swedenborg, at His Second Advent.

The author of this work hopes that he

has faithfully interpreted those wonderful Doctrines which reveal the true meaning of the Lord's Word; and he will be well content if his efforts have stimulated even to a small degree a renewed interest among his readers in that true fountain of all Divine Truth - The Word.

Such daily reading and meditation will not only provide nourishment for our souls-and so assist in our regeneration, but will help to increase the effectiveness of the Church's own witness to the Lord Himself.

The Author

January 1

Creation

"In the beginning God created the heavens and the earth."

> Genesis 1:1

You too, in the beginning, are created heaven and earth: a little spiritual universe. Heaven within and earth without: just as Jesus says in the New Testament "The Kingdom of Heaven is within you"

God creating is the first teaching of the Bible: and the first picture we should have of Him: without Him we can do nothing. Try not to think of time when you think of the beginning: so far as you are concerned it is all NOW. By the beginning is meant the first thing in your creation from which all else follows. First God and Heaven, then earth. You are being created NOW!

Prayer

Create in me a clean heart, O God; and renew a right spirit within me.

Daily Word

January 2

Creation

"And the earth was without form, and void; and darkness was upon the face of the deep."

Genesis 1:2

In our early days we don't think much about heaven. Our earth-life seems nearer to us and much more attractive: in consequence it is out of harmony with heaven. It is spiritually uncultivated, and so is said to be "without form and void." At first our minds are shallow, and their depths are covered with the darkness that arises from ignorance. Soon we must begin to look within, or upward to God our Maker, or our heaven will be disjoined from our earth-life, and we shall become unhappy indeed.

Prayer

O God, be not far from me: O my God, make haste to help me.

January 3

Creation

"And the Spirit of God moved upon the face of the waters."

Genesis 1:2

Water in the Bible is a picture of truth. What water is to natural life truth is to spiritual life. In each case it cleanses and refreshes.

Think of the face of the waters, as the appearance of all the little knowledges of truth that fill your mind. Of themselves they are dead, but when the Spirit of God moves upon them, they awaken and come alive. As they do so you are thrilled with a new delight, and begin to prepare for a new state of spiritual growth or development. These enlivening truths relieve the darkness that covered your mind, and some intelligence begins to remove ignorance.

Prayer

O Lord, withhold not Your tender mercies from me: let Your loving kindness and Your truth continually preserve me.

Daily Word

January 4

Light

"And God said, Let there be light: and there was light. And God saw the light, that it was good: and God divided the light from the darkness."

Genesis 1:3, 4

This is the first kind of light: your mind is now beginning to see and to understand. It is good, because you can now distinguish, if only in a general way, between right and wrong. God has divided the light from the darkness. Now you can begin to look within, or up, to the light: and down to the darkness. Even at this early stage, the choice is before you: there is no compulsion: you can look to the light or to the darkness.

Prayer

O Lord, send out Your light and Your truth: let them lead me; let them bring me to Your holy hill.

January 5

Light

"And God called the light Day, and the darkness he called Night. And the evening and the morning were the first day."

Genesis 1:5

Whatever knowledge of truth is from God, is called Day. There is no night where God is. Whatever is from self, and its own apparent intelligence, is Darkness, and in the Bible is called Night.

When this basic distinction is appreciated and acknowledged, you are at the close of the first stage of your creation into spiritual manhood-the image and likeness of God. The evening and the morning are the first step or day. Thus, the wonderful story of God's Word begins to unfold in your life. The Word is the book of life.

Prayer

Unto You, O Lord, do I lift up my soul. O God I trust in You. Lead me in Your truth, and teach me.

January 6

Light

"And God made two great lights; the greater light to rule the day, and the lesser light to rule the night: he made the stars also."

> Genesis 1:16

What the two great lights-the sun and moon-are to natural life, the two great lights-love and truth-are to spiritual life. The greater light, the sun of heaven, or the Lord's love, rules in our spiritually happy times and the lesser light, the Lord's truth rules in times of spiritual temptations and trial.

Just as the light of the moon is reflected from the sun, and is of itself cold, so truth is reflected from love, and apart from love lacks warmth. In the sun of heaven love and truth are united but in faith only reflected.

Prayer

Be merciful unto us, O God, and bless us; and cause Your face to shine upon us.

Daily Word

January 7

Light

"And Jesus was transfigured before them: and his face did shine as the sun, and his raiment was white as the light."

Matthew 17:2

Even as the sunshine gives us beautiful summer days, so does the warm sunshine of the Lord's love give us summer in our hearts.

We can as it were make our own happy summer by turning to Jesus. Cloudy skies often arise from our self-seeking, but as we try to keep the first commandments of love to the Lord and the neighbour, the clouds open up and His countenance shines upon us again.

You like your house to be in a sunny position: why not build the house of your mind in the sunshine of Divine love?

Prayer

O Lord God, cause Your face to shine; and we shall be saved.

January 8

Light

"Jesus said 'I am the light of the world: he that follows me shall not walk in darkness, but shall have the light of life'."

John 8:12

Though you may not have the means to follow the sun and so avoid the cold dark days of winter, you can follow the spiritual sun. You can leave the cold winter weather of self-seeking: the hard, icy conditions of pride, avarice and unbelief. Without money and without price you can follow the spiritual sun, and delight your soul with goodness. Try it just a little way, and you will be convinced. Follow Jesus and He will fill your own little world with light. Cold and darkness will be scattered, and you will be frost-bound no longer.

Prayer

O Lord, send out your light and your truth: let them lead me.

January 9

Light

"Light has come into the world, and men loved darkness rather than light, because their deeds were evil."

John 3:19

Have you noticed how eagerly evil seeks darkness? How it seeks to hide or cover up what it does? Sometimes by a lie, or pretence, or some other secret hiding place. Like evil beasts it seeks the darkness for its activities. The great destroyer of evil is light. Even daylight robberies are planned in dens of darkness.

Yet how futile it all is! No man can hide himself away from God. The deepest, darkest cavern cannot conceal Him. Read Psalm 139: "If I make my bed in hell, behold, you are there." The love of evil is the love of darkness. Evil and darkness come from hell.

Prayer

O Lord, that art the fountain of life in Your light shall we see light.

January 10

The Garden

"And the Lord God planted a garden eastward in Eden; and there he put the man whom he had formed."

Genesis 2:8

As you grow into spiritual manhood, things of the mind take on a livelier interest. The truth is that God is preparing a garden for you, eastward in your souls, and He is causing you to dress it and keep it. Eastward is where the sun rises; meaning spiritually, where the Lord rises among your good affections and knowledges of Him.

If you like, your mind can now become as Eden, a garden of the Lord. Your affections can be fragrant with His love, in correspondence with the sweetest blooms of an earthly garden: and your thoughts alive from living truth.

Prayer

O Lord, let integrity and uprightness preserve me; for I wait on You.

Daily Word

January 11

The Garden

"The Lord shall comfort Zion and make her wilderness like Eden, and her desert like the garden of the Lord."

Isaiah 51:3

This is spoken of those who follow after righteousness. These are Zion, who is to be comforted and to be filled with joy and gladness. For seeking God's righteousness changes everything. If you are seeking righteousness your mind will soon cultivate knowledges of truth; and good affections will arise where your heart was before like a desert. This wonderful change will come from the Lord, whose comfort is joined together with right thinking and loving.

So, plant the seeds of the Lord's Word in your mind and your wilderness and desert will become like Eden, the garden of the Lord.

Prayer

O God, as the hart pants after the water brooks, so my soul longs after You.

Daily Word

January 12

The Garden

"And the Lord God shall guide you continually, and you shall be like a watered garden."

Isaiah 58:11

Try to believe in the Divine Providence. To do so will give you such happiness. The Lord loves you, and will guide you continually if you will look to Him. Looking to Him means listening to His voice and loving His commandments. He will guide you then, all the way, and bring you safely through all your difficulties.

Your mind will become like a watered garden, full of colour, and rich with fruit. It will be a mind where the Lord can walk and communicate with you.

Prayer

Hear me, when I call, O God of my righteousness: have mercy upon me and hear my prayer. You have put gladness in my heart.

Daily Word

January 13

Serpents

"Now the serpent was more subtle than any beast of the field which the Lord God had made."

Genesis 3:1

Unexpectedly, with subtle guile, the serpent stole into Eden long ago. In the Bible the serpent represents evil of every kind, but particularly sensual evil. In you, it is that which would turn you from God to your own desires, and your own judgement of good and evil. This principle, like the serpent, is subtle, and moves quietly among your lowest appetites waiting its opportunity to deceive. It wants everything to serve its own gratification. It lives on the dust.

The Lord stands at the door knocking. If you listen to His voice, you will have strength to overcome the serpent.

Prayer

In You O Lord, do I put my trust: let me never be put to confusion.

Daily Word

January 14

Serpents

"And the Lord God said to the woman, What is this that you have done? And the woman said, The serpent beguiled me, and I ate."

Genesis 3:13

For what you do, you are responsible! In your choice you have the freedom. of manhood. This woman listened to the serpent, and freely chose to do its bidding. When the inevitable trouble followed, she blamed the serpent. But even in this she was actually blaming herself, for the serpent represented her sensual nature. When we once yield to our lower nature it casts us out of Eden, and it is quite a long way back. But we can return, for Jesus comes to seek and to save the lost.

Prayer

Deliver me from blood guiltiness, O God, You God of my salvation: and my tongue shall sing aloud of Your righteousness.

Daily Word

January 15

Serpents

"The wolf and the lamb shall feed together, and the lion shall eat straw like the bullock: and dust shall be the serpent's meat. They shall not hurt nor destroy in all my holy mountain, says the Lord."

Isaiah 65:25

This is such a happy picture. The holy mountain of the Lord is the country of his holy love. The serpent, representing our sensual nature is still a part of us, and can even have a good signification when it is properly subservient to our spiritual manhood.

Dust, the nourishment of mere appetite, is still its meat but in its proper place it does not hurt nor destroy. The spiritual principle should always control the natural.

Prayer

Withhold not You Your tender mercies from me, O Lord: let Your loving kindness and Your truth continually preserve me.

Daily Word

January 16

The Tree

"And the Lord God commanded the man, saying, Of every tree of the garden you may freely eat: But of the tree of the knowledge of good and evil, you shall not eat: for in the day that you eat of it you shall surely die."

Genesis 2:16, 17

Why is the fruit of this one tree forbidden? Simply because it is so deadly. By feeding upon it is meant that we make our own standards of good and evil: and our own standards arise from the love of self. If you follow your self-hood instead of God, you will spiritually die. God is the Maker of heaven and earth and all the laws of life: without Him you can do nothing.

Prayer

Hear my prayer, O Lord, and let my cry come to You. Hide not Your face from me in the day when I am in trouble.

January 17

The Tree

"To him that overcomes will I give to eat of the tree of life, which is in the midst of the paradise of God."

Revelation 2:7

To eat of the tree of life is to feed on the Lord's goodness and truth. In another place (chap. 22) we read that this tree yielded her fruit every month: that is, for every succeeding state of faith. Its leaves also are for the healing of the nations: they are the truths of good through which it breathes. This wonderful tree is in the midst of the garden, the paradise of God. If you overcome putting self first, by loving God first, then you will eat of this tree of life.

Prayer

O Lord, I have longed for Your salvation, and Your law is my delight. Let my soul live, and it shall praise You.

January 18

The Tree

"Blessed is the man that trusts in the Lord
he shall be as a tree planted by the waters,
and that spreads out her roots by the river,
and shall not die when heat comes, but her
leaf shall be green."

Jeremiah 17:7, 8

To be blessed is to be happy: and the greatest happiness comes to those who trust in the Lord. They are compared in the Bible to trees planted by waters that in consequence flourish: and the leaves are always green.

To trust in the Lord is to trust all the way: not just for those few steps you can see, but for all the subsequent steps as well. Thus, we become trees of the Lord.

Prayer

Be merciful to me, O God, be merciful to me: for my soul trusts in You: yes, in the shadow of Your wings will I make my refuge.

Daily Word

January 19

The Ark

"And the flood was forty days upon the earth; and the waters increased, and bare up the ark, and it was lift up above the earth."

Genesis 7:17

Floods in the Bible stand for something more than just floods of water: spiritually they represent a flood of false ideas and temptations. Just as they affect multitudes of people, so they happen to individuals.

The ark represents the Lord, or the Lord's provision that you may be saved. It is that little good, hidden deep in the heart, prepared by the Divine Providence, perhaps from earliest days: something good and innocent that flooding temptation cannot drown: something the floods will bear up above the earth. It is your most precious gift from God.

Prayer

O Lord, quicken me for Your name's sake: for Your righteousness' sake bring my soul out of trouble.

Daily Word

January 20

The Ark

"She took for him an ark of bulrushes, and daubed it with slime and with pitch, and put the child therein; and she laid it in the flags by the river's brink."

Exodus 2:3

The child in the ark is Moses. Moses represents the law of the Lord. Pharaoh was afraid of the children of Israel and arranged that all baby boys should be drowned. But the Divine Providence overruled evil and provided a means of escape for Moses, who later led Israel out of bondage.

The ark is a picture of something good provided by love. If you have a little love for the Lord's teaching, it will lift you above the evil river: and eventually lead you to heaven.

Prayer

O Lord, attend to my cry: for I am brought very low: O Lord deliver me from my persecutors.

January 21

The Ark

"And you shall put the mercy seat above upon the ark; and in the ark you shall put the testimony that I shall give you."

Exodus 25:21

This ark containing the commandments was the most holy thing in the tabernacle of the Children of Israel. It was covered by the mercy seat, and above, with wings outspread, were two cherubim.

In an individual sense you are a church or tabernacle in particular. Inwardly in the tabernacle of your soul is the secret place where God communes with you. Here is the ark, or knowledge of heavenly things, where God and His commandments are sacred. As we follow the ark we go forward on our journey to the Promised Land.

Prayer

O Lord, send out Your light and Your truth: let them lead me: let them bring me into Your Holy hill.

January 22

Stones

"And they said let us make brick, and they had brick for stone and slime for mortar. And they said, "Let us go and build a city and a tower, whose top may reach up to heaven; and let us make us a name, lest we be scattered."

Genesis 11:3, 4

These people substituted brick for stone, and slime for mortar; hoping to build themselves a way up to heaven, and make themselves a name. Their purpose and practice were bad and they soon came to confusion.

You and I make the same mistake when we imagine we can climb up to heaven by our own intelligence. We substitute brick for stone, when we make artificial truth; and slime for mortar, when we bind our bricks with self-indulgence.

Prayer

Hear, O Lord, and have mercy upon me:
Lord, be You my helper.

Daily Word

January 23

Stones

"Jesus said, Have ye not read this scripture; The stone which the builders rejected is become the cornerstone: this was the Lord's doing, and it is marvellous in our eyes."

Mark 12:10, 11

It is obvious that stones in the Bible represent truth or truths-sometimes the opposite. But those who do not love the Lord reject His truth.

Would you like to build the house of your soul on a secure foundation, so that it can withstand all the storms and adversities of life? You can do so! But you must not reject the Lord and His teachings. You must build on His truths and make Him the head of the corner.

Prayer

O Lord, be You my strong habitation, where unto I may continually resort; for You are my rock and my fortress.

January 24

Stones

"And the foundations of the wall of the city were garnished with all manner of precious stones."

Revelation 21:19

This picture of the holy city is entrancing: jasper walls, golden streets, gates of pearl, and foundations of precious stones. And within, in the midst, the tree of life.

It is a picture of the Lord's church, not in any narrow or sectarian sense, but of His universal church in heaven and earth. It is founded on all manner of precious stones-all the precious truths of His Word. All who love the Lord and keep His commandments may enter in-even you and I.

The gates are never closed.

Prayer

O Lord, Your hands have made me and fashioned me: give me understanding, that I may learn Your commandments.

Daily Word

January 25

Journeys

"Now the Lord had said to Abram, Get you out of your country, and from your kindred, and from your father's house, to a land that I will show you."

Genesis 12:1

What the Lord says to Abram, He says to us all. It is a call to the good within us, to journey away from the country of self-love, to the country of the Lord.

Our kindred represent our merely worldly associates, and our father's house the old Adam of self-love. The land He will show us is Canaan, which signifies Heaven and our life there. We do not know the way and we cannot see the place, but His providence will direct us safely to it.

Prayer

O Lord, send out Your light and Your truth, let them lead me; let them bring me unto Your holy hill.

January 26

Journeys

"And it came to pass, that, while they communed together and reasoned, Jesus himself drew near, and went with them."

Luke 24:15

Two friends of Jesus were on a little journey to Emmaus. While they walked along, talking, a stranger joined them. "What are you talking of? Why are you sad?" the stranger asked. They told him of Jesus who had been crucified and Who they now heard was alive again.

It is good, as you journey on the road, to meditate and to talk together of Jesus. His providence will cover you as you walk along: and though you know it not He may Join you unawares.

Prayer

Let the words of my mouth, and the meditation of my heart, be acceptable in Your sight, O Lord, my strength, and my redeemer.

Daily Word

January 27

Journeys

"And not many days after the younger son gathered all together, and took his journey into a far country, and there wasted his substance with riotous living."

Luke 15:13

This poor boy took his journey away from home, to the far country of self-gratification; and in consequence he was soon lost. This involved another journey, for when he came to himself, he saw he must return home. The journey home was harder, for it meant repentance and humiliation. But it also meant his Father's love, and his Father's home; and no more bitterness and hunger.

Prayer

O Lord, look upon my affliction and my pain: and forgive me all my sins. For I put my trust in You.

January 28

Bread

"Then said the Lord to Moses, Behold, I will rain bread from heaven for you. And when the children of Israel saw it, they said one to another, It is manna: for they knew not what it was."

Exodus 16:4 & 15

The people journeying through the wilderness were hungry, and God sent them bread from heaven. When they found it on the ground, and gathered it morning by morning they said, "It is manna," meaning they did not know what it was.

It is really a picture of ourselves on our journey from this world to heaven. God sends us bread, not only for our bodies but also for our souls. He sends just enough each morning for our need. It is manna! We do not understand it, but it happens just the same.

Prayer

O Lord, be You our refuge and strength, a very present help in trouble.

Daily Word

January 29

Bread

"Most assuredly, I say to you, he that believes in me has everlasting life. I am that bread of life."

John 6:47, 48

How very important it is to believe in the one we love. And it is of the very greatest importance to believe in God, whom the first commandment bids us love with all our heart. Indeed, to believe lovingly in the Lord is to have everlasting life. But to have life of any kind we must have food. The body cannot live without it, neither can the soul. Jesus tells us this, for when He speaks of everlasting life, He says, "I am that bread of life."

To feed on this bread is to believe in Him and love Him.

Prayer

Let Your mercy, O Lord, be upon us, according as we hope in You.

Daily Word

January 30

Bread

"He that has an ear, let him hear what the Spirit says to the churches; To him that overcomes will I give to eat of the hidden manna."

Revelation 2:17

It is easier to listen to the sounds of this world than to the voice of the Lord in His Word. But it is important that we make an effort to hear the Lord's voice, because then we can open the door, and He will come in and sup with us. To this end we must overcome the predominant voice of the world. As we do so we shall be blessed with hidden manna: supping with Jesus we shall feed on His love, and be nourished secretly in our souls.

Prayer

O Lord, You are my rock and my fortress: therefore for Your name's sake lead me, and guide me.

January 31

Clouds

"And the Lord went before them by day in a pillar of cloud, to lead them the way."

Exodus 13:21

The story of the children of Israel journeying through the wilderness is full of interest and significance. On our way from the bondage of self-love, to the love of God and our neighbour, we are ever led by the Lord's love. But we do not easily see that it is love leading us. The love is hidden in the commandments and laws of the journey, and is often obscure: and so we are led by a pillar of cloud. Like the Israelites we often fret, but the Divine Providence understands and brings us safely home.

Prayer

O Lord, make me to go in the path of Your commandments; for therein do I delight.

February 1

Clouds

"O Lord my God, you are very great who makes the clouds his chariot: who walks upon the wings of the wind."

Psalm 104:1, 3

The Lord riding in clouds! At first this may seem strange. Yet almost all of our experience confirms this idea. Do you remember your early school days? How obscure arithmetic and spelling were! Every new little truth you had to learn came in a cloud. It is just the same with Bible truth. It all has to be learned. Even to those advanced in religious life many Bible passages are dark, and many seem as contradictions. Actually, they are full of love and light. The truths of the Word are the clouds of heaven - the chariot of the Lord.

Prayer

O Lord, let Your tender mercies come to me, that I may live: for Your law is my delight.

Daily Word

February 2

Clouds

"And they shall see the Son of man coming in the clouds of heaven with power and great glory."

Matthew 24:30

Often when we suffer trials and temptations we come into great distress. Then life seems dark and impossible, but the Lord mercifully shortens those days for us, by turning our thoughts to Him. We begin to read His Word, and to seek Him there: things that before seemed dark and cold light up. Here and there the sun of love warms and cheers us. Then the Son of man comes in power and great glory-comes to you and me-in the truths, or clouds of His Word.

Prayer

Be merciful to me, O God, for my soul trusts in You. Your mercy is great unto the heavens, and Your truth unto the clouds.

February 3

River Jordan

"Behold, the ark of the covenant of the Lord of all the earth passes over before you into Jordan."

Joshua 3:11

Roughly, the River Jordan divided the wilderness from the Promised Land. It was the last obstacle to the children of Israel on their journey from Egypt to Canaan.

When we follow the Lord's commandments, represented by the ark of the covenant, we eventually cross Jordan into the Holy Land. Jordan represents the Lord's Word: the dividing line between heaven and earth. Its natural sense introduces us to the spiritual within, where the Lord dwells. Thus, the commandments lead us to eternal love.

Prayer

Hear, O Lord, when I cry with my voice: have mercy also upon me, and answer me. When You said, Seek ye my face; my heart said, Your face, Lord, will I seek.

February 4

River Jordan

"Then went Naaman down, and dipped himself seven times in Jordan, according to the saying of the man of God: and his flesh came again like the flesh of a little child, and he was clean."

2 Kings 5:14

This story of Naaman and the little captive maid, with the visit to Elisha, stirs the imagination. Here is disease, pride, a long journey, and a picture of healing and humility.

Naaman may represent you: Elisha the prophet represents the Lord: leprosy corresponds to profanation. You go to the Lord to be healed, and you are told to wash seven times in Jordan. When you do so, you are clean, for the waters of Jordan represent the cleansing truths of the Lord's Word.

Prayer

Have mercy upon me, O God, according to Your loving kindness: wash me thoroughly from my iniquity, and cleanse me from my sin.

Daily Word

February 5

River Jordan

"Then went out to John, Jerusalem and all Judaea, and all the region round about Jordan, and were baptised of him in Jordan, confessing their sins."

Matthew 3:5, 6

If you are interested in a vigorous religion, go into the wilderness of Judaea, and listen to John Baptist. He is young and austere, clothed in camel's hair and eating insects, locusts and wild honey. His message is direct and quite unflattering. He is, indeed, a voice crying in the wilderness, calling to repentance.

John is introducing and preparing the way for Jesus, just as the literal story of the Bible does. He baptises in the waters of Jordan, because they, like the truths of the Word, give entrance to heaven and the Lord Himself.

Prayer

Hear me when I call, O God of my righteousness: have mercy upon me, and hear my prayer.

Daily Word

February 6

Wilderness

"Behold, I will do a new thing; now it shall spring forth; shall ye not know it? I will even make a way in the wilderness, and rivers in the desert."

Isaiah 43:19

A way in the wilderness gives access, and rivers allow gardens to replace the desert. Together, they make a great and notable change.

There comes a time for many of us when we begin to realise that our minds are not unlike a wilderness, and that our hearts are desert-like. What can we do about it? Well, the Lord has said, "I am the way". If we follow Him, He will make a way through: and where our hearts are parched, rivers of truth will turn them into gardens of the Lord.

Prayer

Let Your mercies come also to me, O Lord, even Your salvation, according to Your Word.

Daily Word

February 7

Commandments

"O that You had listened to my commandments! Then had your peace been as a river, and your righteousness as the waves of the sea."

Isaiah 48:18

Many people do not like the commandments: others try to by-pass them. Yet Jesus said that those who loved Him were those that kept His commandments. We must recognise that all the regulations of the Lord are given out of love, and for the sake of love. When we follow, they guide our feet into the way of peace. He who breaks the least of them, Jesus said, would be called the least in heaven.

The Commandments lead us beside the still waters; the deep, quiet truths of the Word, flowing into peace.

Prayer

I cried, O Lord, with my whole heart; hear me and help me, for all Your commandments are truth.

Daily Word

February 8

Rivers

"And he showed me a pure river of water of life, clear as crystal, proceeding out of the throne of God and of the Lamb."

Revelation 22:1

You have seen the river flowing under the bridge in the town. You have, perhaps, walked along its banks. Have you seen the other river, pure and clear as crystal? It flows from the throne of God; its waters are the waters of life. It is the river of holy truth, alive from the love of God. You can see it in the Bible, flowing down from heaven to earth. It is composed of all the truths or teachings of the Lord. You walk along its banks when you read the Word.

Prayer

O Lord, satisfy us early with Your mercy: that we may rejoice and be glad all our days.

February 9

Choosing

"Choose you this day whom ye will serve; but as for me and my house, we will serve the Lord."

> Joshua 24:15

To be able to choose! This is something we all value. Yet, when we think of it, we see it makes us responsible: and it is easy to make a mistake.

Joshua knew that he could not force the Israelites to follow this or that course. They, like us, had to choose to follow their own way, or the Lord's. But having made their choice, they alone were responsible. Nevertheless, Joshua gave them inspiration and an example. "As for me and my house," he said, "we will serve the Lord."

Prayer

O Lord, one thing have I desired, that I will seek after: that I may dwell in the house of the Lord all the days of my life.

February 10

Choosing

"One thing is needful: and Mary has chosen that good part, which shall not be taken away from her."

Luke 10:42

This is another quite different picture of choosing. It is not so much one of choosing a way to take, but rather of choosing what to do when Jesus is a guest in the house.

From an individual point of view the house maybe you: you as to your mind. Then it would be you who invited Jesus in. Martha may represent your thoughts busily. active, thinking of ways to serve. But Mary would represent your love so warmed and happy by the presence of Jesus that it could choose nothing else than to sit and listen to Him.

Prayer

Hear me, O Lord; for your loving kindness is good: turn to me according to the multitude of your tender mercies.

Daily Word

February 11

Choosing

"Multitudes, multitudes in the valley of decision: for the day of the Lord is near in the valley of decision."

Joel 3:14

Decision, or deciding, is choosing. There are always multitudes of people faced with the need of decision. The valley is a picture of the cleft between two opposing positions: it is here that men become conscious of the necessity of choosing: and of their freedom of choice.

In your life the multitudes are your thronging thoughts and feelings. The valley of decision is the free place between right and wrong, where your choice must be made. The Lord is always near in the freedom of your mind. Call upon Him, while He is near.

Prayer

Lord, there be many that say, who will show us any good? O Lord, lift up the light of Your countenance upon us.

Daily Word

February 12

Rain

"My doctrine shall drop as the rain, my speech shall distil as the dew, as the small rain upon the tender herb, and as the showers upon the grass."

Deuteronomy 32:2

Just as the rain refreshes and blesses the earth, so the teachings of the Lord drop their loving blessings on His children. And His sayings distil their tenderness on all who receive them. The small rain, suited to the young or tender seedling, pictures the gentle blessings of loving kindness that fall about us in the early days of Christian experience. Showers on the grass, causing it to be green and fresh, are like the Lord's blessings enlivening our simple earliest knowledge of Him.

Prayer

O Lord, the earth is full of Your mercy: teach me Your statutes. Your hands have made me; give me understanding, that I may learn Your commandments.

Daily Word

February 13

Rain

"For as the rain comes down, and the snow from heaven, and returns not there, but waters the earth ... so shall my word be that goes forth out of my mouth: it shall not return to me void."

Isaiah 55:10, 11

Here, the Lord likens the falling of rain to the words of His mouth. As rain waters the earth and causes growth, so His words or teaching prosper His purpose. Those who receive His blessings will go out with joy and be led forth in peace. Where the Lord's Word is received it always bears fruit: it does not return void.

Prayer

Hear me, O Lord; for Your loving kindness is good: turn unto me according to the multitude of Your tender mercies. And hide not Your face from Your servant.

Daily Word

February 14

Rain

"And the rain descended, and the floods came, and the winds blew, and beat upon that house; and it fell not: for it was founded upon a rock."

Matthew 7:25

This is said of wise folk, who hear and do the Lord's sayings; who Jesus says build on a rock.

Rain, in a good sense, signifies blessings of truth and good from the Lord's love. But in an opposite sense, it represents floods of false and evil affections, from the love of self and the world. But when we build on the rock of the Lord's teaching, we are able to withstand all the attacks of our fallen nature.

Prayer

O Lord, order my steps in Your word: and let not any iniquity have dominion over me. Deliver me from the oppression of evil: so will I keep Your precepts.

Daily Word

February 15

Commandments

"O how I love your law! It is my meditation all the day. Through Your commandments You have made me wiser than my enemies: for they are ever with me."

Psalm 119:97, 98

The Commandments and our enemies!
The commandments are God's regulations for a wise and happy life. They are the road to the life that is lived in heaven. Internally they are the love that is God.

The enemies that are ever with us are the feelings and thoughts that are concerned only with the love we have for ourselves. These are real enemies, ever trying to pull us away from the Lord and heaven. All our unhappiness is caused by them.

Prayer

In You, O Lord, do I put my trust: let me never be put to confusion. Deliver me in Your righteousness, and cause me to escape.

Daily Word

February 16

Commandments

"And Jesus answered him, The first of all the commandments is, Hear, O Israel; The Lord our God is one Lord: and you shall love the Lord your God with all your heart, and with all your soul, and with all your mind, and with all your strength."

Mark 12:29, 30

All the teachings and commands of the Lord are summed up in this first and great commandment. To apply it to life is to be conjoined to the Lord. It is to live as He teaches.

It simply means, that we are to be devoted to His will, with all the strength of our love and understanding. Then, also, we will really love our neighbour.

Prayer

Search me, O God, and know my heart: try me, and know my thoughts: and see if there be any wicked way in me.

Daily Word

February 17

Commandments

"A new commandment I give unto you, That ye love one another; as I have loved you, that ye also love one another. By this shall all men know that ye are my disciples."

John 13:34, 35

This is the rule Jesus gives us by which men shall know us to be His disciples. It is the rule of Divine Love. But most of us find it very exacting. What happy people we would be, if we lived as the Lord teaches!
To love others as Jesus loves us, is to love them outside of self-interest. It is to love them regardless of their love for us. It is to love their welfare and seek their good.

Prayer

O Lord, Your hands have made me and fashioned me: give me understanding, that I, may learn Your commandments.

February 18

Oil

"And you shall command the children of Israel, that they bring you pure olive oil beaten for the light, to cause the lamp to burn always."

Exodus 27:20

Olive oil has an important place in the Bible story. It was used by the people for heating and lighting and for healing. But its great importance in the Lord's Word is in the spiritual significance; every use olive oil supplied naturally has its spiritual correspondence. Olive oil, in general, is a picture of love. Love warms your hearts, and the light arising from love lights the rooms of your mind. Love heals and soothes spiritual ailments. Love causes the lamp of life to burn always.

Prayer

O Lord, help us to remember always that Your Word is a lamp unto our feet and a light to our path.

Daily Word

February 19

Oil

"You love righteousness, and hate wickedness: therefore, God, your God, has anointed you with the oil of gladness above your fellows."

Psalm 45:7

The Lord makes His sun of love to shine on the evil equally with the good: but evil does not receive it as good does. Reception makes all the difference. The love of righteousness opens all the doors of the heart and understanding: when these are opened gladness enters deeply. To be anointed with the oil of gladness is to be blessed with the delight of love. Above our fellows, here means, as the text implies, above what would be possible if we did not love righteousness.

Prayer

Keep me, O Lord, from the hands of the wicked; preserve me from the violent man; who have purposed to overthrow my goings.

Daily Word

February 20

Oil

"And five of them were wise, and five were foolish. They that were foolish took their lamps and took no oil with them: but the wise took oil in their vessels with their lamps."

Matthew 25:2, 3, 4

The wise and the foolish! It is a picture of ourselves. We all have lamps, but some of us do not provide oil. Lamps signify the truths that form our faith. But, like lamps without oil, so is faith without love. We cannot be saved by faith alone. As lamps need oil, so faith needs love. Love burns warmly, and gives a light to our path. Love in our faith numbers us with the wise.

Prayer

O Lord, make Your Word a lamp unto my feet, and a light unto my path: for it is the rejoicing of my heart.

February 21

Lamps

"And the child Samuel ministered to the Lord before Eli and there the lamp of God went out in the temple of the Lord, where the ark of God was, and Samuel was laid down to sleep the Lord called Samuel."

1 Samuel 3:1, 3, 4

This is one of the Bible stories many of us remember from childhood - the child Samuel: the little light from the lamp: the sacred ark containing the commandments; and in the night the unseen voice, calling, "Samuel, Samuel".

Samuel may be a picture of you trying to serve the Lord. The lamp alight in the temple, represents the Lord's love-warm and bright. The unseen voice is that of the Lord in His Word calling you. Can you respond, Speak Lord, for your servant hears?

Prayer

O Lord, my light and my salvation, leave me not, neither forsake me.

Daily Word

February 22

Lamps

"Your word is a lamp unto my feet, and a light unto my path."

Psalm 119:105

There are many kinds of lamps, lanterns and lights, from the powerful lamp of the lighthouse to the little night-light in its saucer of water. Almost always they give cheer and comfort.

But how is the Lord's Word a lamp? It is a lamp because it is filled with the oil of love. It is a light, because from God's love comes all the light of life. Your feet, are the part of your body that is most continuously in contact with the earth: they represent your natural life. The light of the Lord's Word falls on your daily life and shows you how to tread.

Prayer

O Lord, show us Your mercy, and grant us Your salvation and set us in the path of Your steps.

Daily Word

February 23

Lamps

"For you will light my candle: the Lord my God will enlighten my darkness."

> Psalm 18:28

We all need light. In the winter how often we look forward to the summer, when it is light from early morning till bedtime.

We all need spiritual light too. Without it, our minds become progressively darker and the gladness of life dies away. Just as when the earth turns nearer to the sun, summer with its warmth and light comes again; so when we turn to the Lord, His love fills our minds with light.

He lights our candle and enlightens our darkness. In the light He gives, we can enter into all the delight of spiritual summer.

Prayer

Consider and hear, me, O Lord my God; lighten my eyes, lest I sleep the sleep of death.

February 24

Chastening

"Lord, how are they increased that trouble me! Many are they that rise up against me."

Psalm 3:1

Sometimes it seems that everything goes wrong. Trouble increases, and more difficulties rise up against us. In periods like this we may come into states approaching despair. We do not know at the time that great good may come to us by way of these afflictions.

You see, they turn our thoughts to the Lord and away from ourselves. They chasten and humble us and direct us to a happier way of life. Usually, in troubled times we blame others, and circumstances; but we have to learn that, more often than not, troubles arise from pride, self-confidence and self-love: these are our enemies.

Prayer

Arise, O Lord; save me, O my God: for You smite my enemies upon the cheek bone.

Daily Word

February 25

Chastening

"Depart from me, all ye workers of iniquity; for the Lord has heard the voice of my weeping. The Lord has heard my supplication."

Psalm 6:8, 9

Go away! Go away! How often you and I have spoken like this to selfish promptings. Selfish promptings are workers of iniquity. When we indulge them our happiness departs, and we are soon In danger of destruction.

Frequently it is not easy to send them away: then is the time to seek help from the Lord; to cry out to Him in our need. He will hear the voice of our distress, and our prayers for aid: then we will be able successfully to tell the workers of iniquity to depart.

Prayer

Have mercy upon me, O Lord; for I am weak: O Lord, heal me; for I am sore vexed.

Daily Word

February 26

Chastening

"It is God that avenges me, and subdues the people under me. He delivers me from my enemies: yea, you lift me up above those that rise up against me."

Psalm 18:47, 48

Think of the people to be subdued under you as the crowds of false ideas that would like to take control; and of the enemies as the evil and selfish indulgences that could destroy your soul. And acknowledge that evil of every kind should always be below your feet.

Then you will understand what is meant by God's subduing the people under you, and delivering you from your enemies; and that He lifts you up above these things.

Prayer

O Lord, deliver me from my enemies; lift me up above those that rise up against me, and save me.

Daily Word

February 27

Wheat and Tares

"Let both grow together until the harvest: and in the time of harvest I will say to the reapers, Gather ye together first the tares, and bind them in bundles to burn them: but gather the wheat into my barn."

Matthew 13:30

In this passage it is possible to see our lives as in a mirror. When we look carefully into ourselves we can see many false things together with good ones.

Sometimes we may wonder whether the tares will ever be overcome; but the Lord says, "Let both grow together until the harvest"; it is a part of His merciful providence.

At last when our characters are judged the angels will gather together all that is false and destroy it, but all our wheat will be saved.

Prayer

Unto you, O Lord, do I lift up my soul.

Daily Word

February 28

Foes

"A man's foes shall be they of his own household."

Matthew 10:36

The Lord teaches us to honour father and mother and to love others as ourselves. At first then, it seems strange that He should tell us that our enemies are in our own household.

But in Bible language, your household means yours! Your very own, for even if you live alone in a cave, you still have a household. Your house is your mind.

The family of your mind is composed of all your nearest and dearest desires, and all your teeming thoughts. Among these are many that are selfish and false; these are your true foes: your dangerous enemies!

Prayer

O Lord, consider my enemies; for they are many: O keep my soul, and deliver me: for I put my trust in You.

Daily Word

February 29

The horrible pit

"He brought me up also out of a horrible pit, out of the miry clay, and set my feet upon a rock, and established my goings."

Psalm 40:2

A horrible pit, signifies self-esteem, which sinks down into hell. Miry clay signifies the lusts of selfishness, which adhere to us with sickening tenacity.

Our feet correspond to our natural life, which is in almost constant contact with worldly things. As we humbly approach the Lord our natural life is brought up: lifted up out of the pit of devastation; till our activities on the natural plane are made secure on the rock of the Lord's commandments.

Thus our goings are established, and we shall reach heaven at the end of the road.

Prayer

Be merciful to me, O God, deliver my feet from falling, that I may walk before You in the night of the living.

Daily Word

March 1

The Lord

"In you, O Lord, do I put my trust: let me never be put to confusion: ... Be you my strong habitation, where I may continually resort: you have given commandment to save me; for you are my rock and my fortress."

Psalm 71:1, 3

The Lord's strong habitation is His love. He tells us in John 15: "If ye keep my commandments ye shall abide in my love." Not only is the strong habitation His love, but it is also founded on His wisdom, the rock of eternal truth. These, His love and truth together, provide a fortress no enemy within or without can overthrow. Find this fortress and you will never be put to confusion.

Prayer

I am poor and needy:, make haste to me, O God: You are my help and my deliverer; O Lord, make no tarrying.

Daily Word

March 2

The Lord

"Blessed be the Lord my strength, which teaches my hands to war, and my fingers to fight: my goodness, and my fortress; my high tower, and my deliverer; my shield and he in whom I trust; who subdues my people under me."

Psalm 144:1, 2

When we once really know that of ourselves we can do nothing, we begin to find wisdom. Then we accept the teaching of the Lord, and draw all our strength from Him. We tackle the enemies arising from self-love with new purpose and vigour and much more successfully. The Lord's eternal truth becomes a high tower of defence shielding us from the enemy on every side.

Prayer

Bring my soul, O Lord, out of prison, that I may praise Your name: let the righteous compass me about; and deal bountifully with me.

March 3

The Lord

"The Lord is my light and my salvation; whom shall I fear? The Lord is the strength of my life; of whom shall I be afraid?"

Psalm 27:1

The Lord's light shines out from infinite love. When we accept this light we do not walk in darkness, but into everlasting life. This true salvation, from all the horrors of self-love, pride and destroying appetites, is of the Lord alone. In fallowing Him we have nothing to fear. We may be frail but He is strong: underneath us are the everlasting arms; and the hands that built heaven and earth can hold us securely in every trial. He is our strength every moment. Of whom can we be afraid?

Prayer

O Lord, You have been my help; leave me not, neither forsake me, O God of my salvation.

March 4

The Lord

"The Lord is my shepherd; I shall not want. He makes me to lie down in green pastures."

Psalm 23:1, 2

The twenty-third Psalm is known and loved all over the Christian world. To be able to say in one's own heart, "The Lord is my shepherd", is to experience one of the greatest blessings. It is our acknowledgement of Divine providence, leading, sheltering, feeding, all along the way to our Father's home. There is nothing we can want above this: there are green pastures to rest in, and loving wise provision for every need, every step of the way. The green pastures are, of course, the refreshing restful teachings of the Lord's Word; to rest in these, is indeed to be restored in heart and soul.

Prayer

O Lord, our Shepherd, be You our refuge and strength, a very present help in trouble.

Daily Word

March 5

The Shepherd

"He shall feed his flock like a shepherd: he shall gather the lambs with his arm, and carry them in his bosom, and shall gently lead those that are with young."

Isaiah 40:11

How beautiful this is! The Lord, the Shepherd; His flock, those who follow Him: fed daily by His hands. More closely and interiorly the flock is the group of good affections and thoughts in your mind: those that fallow the Shepherd's voice. And the lambs are the little innocent treasures, perhaps stored up from long ago: these the Good Shepherd carries very tenderly with wonderful care. And your heart that is holding new seedlings of love for Jesus, is led very gently with infinite patience.

Prayer

O Lord, be merciful to us and bless us; and cause Your face to shine upon us.

March 6

The Shepherd

"I am the good shepherd, and know my sheep, and am known of mine."

John 10:14

What we love we call good. The Lord is the Good Shepherd because He is love; because He loves us, and His sheep love Him.

Love knows and understands more wisely than anything else. The Good Shepherd knows His sheep. He knows you, not superficially but absolutely and thoroughly: just how far you can be led today, and just when you must rest on the way. It is because of His love and knowledge that He is able to lead you so perfectly. As you accept and follow His leading you, too, come to know Him and in His leading find increasing delight.

Prayer

In You, O Lord, do I put my trust: let me never be put to confusion.

March 7

Providence

"Surely goodness and mercy shall follow me all the days of my life: and I will dwell in the house of the Lord for ever."

Psalm 23:6

This is a picture of providence, and of its gentle leading. Because we are able to look back, and see something of the wonder of its leading, it is said to follow us. For though we cannot see anything of providence even a little way ahead, the days that are past reveal its goodness and mercy. We learn to listen for the Shepherd's voice: we know that if we follow it will lead us home and that we will dwell there forever.

Mercy hides tomorrow's difficulties; and mercy following gives us assurance day by day.

Prayer

O Lord, cause me to hear Your loving kindness in the morning; for in you do I trust.

Daily Word

March 8

Walking with the Lord

"What does the Lord require of you, but to do justly, and to love mercy, and to walk humbly with your God?"

Micah 6:8

This passage might be used as an illustration of how to keep the first two great commandments; of love to the Lord and love to the neighbour.

The man who does justly, loves mercy, and walks humbly with the Lord, loves the Lord with his heart and mind. He also loves his neighbour as himself. Justice, mercy and humility are the true signs - the actual signs-of Christian life. They are the three qualities the Lord requires of you and of me. Justice is good, mercy is gentle, humility is wise.

Prayer

O Lord, make me to go in the path of Your commandments; for therein do I delight.

March 9

The Lord

"You are my portion, O Lord: I have said that
I would keep your words. The earth, O Lord,
is full of your mercy: teach me your
statutes."

Psalm 119:57, 64

If you keep the Lord's words you will be numbered among the happy. You will experience mercy in your heaven within, and also in your earth life without.

Your daily activities so concerned with the things of the world, and often of the earth, earthy, will nevertheless be full of the Lord's mercies. Mercy will soften every hardship and ease all your problems. It will enable you to forgive in juries, bear sorrows, and to love your fellow men. So make the Lord your portion.

Prayer

O Lord, let Your tender mercies come unto me, that I may live: for Your law is my delight.

March 10

Praise

"Make a joyful noise to God, all ye lands:
Sing forth the honour of His name; make his praise glorious."

Psalm 66:1, 2

The natural land has its own way of making a joyful noise to its Maker. Mountains and hills: streams and rivers: flowers and fruit: flight and songs of birds: sunrise and sunset: blue skies and stars; all proclaim His glory.

How does the land of your life make its joyful noise? By keeping the Lord's teachings: for then all your activities shout His praises. The duties of your calling, your energy and interest in public service, your patient kindliness and understanding, all praise His name. And men seeing your good works glorify with you, your Father in heaven.

Prayer

O Lord, with my whole heart have I sought You: O let me not wander from Your commandments.

Daily Word

March 11

Praise

"Let everything that has breath praise the Lord. Praise ye the Lord."

Psalm 150:6

This is the mountain top of the Psalms: the very last verse, the crown of praise! Here, all the wonder and the beauty of the Book of Psalms is summed up in praise. Let everything that has breath praise the Lord. Spiritually understood, "breath" is the spirit of the Lord's teachings-the truth breathed upon mankind from His love. And we read, "Jesus breathed on His disciples and says, Receive ye the Holy Spirit." All who receive this blessing have "breath": and all who receive it praise the Lord. Everything in your life that breathes from Him, praises the Lord.

Prayer

Bless the Lord, O my soul. O Lord my God, You are very great; You are clothed with honour and majesty.

March 12

Praise

"Amen: Blessing, and glory, and wisdom, and thanksgiving, and honour, and power, and might, be to our God for ever and ever, Amen."

Revelation 7:12

"**A**men" signifies confirmation. It is almost like saying, "Yes, yes!" And here, although it seems as though the angels, or perhaps ourselves, are giving blessing and glory to the Lord, it is only an appearance: we having nothing to give. We appear to ourselves to give when we receive; for in receiving we acknowledge before Him that all is His. All the blessings of glory and wisdom, all the thanksgiving and honour and power and might are His for ever and ever. Amen!

Prayer

O Lord, how manifold are Your works! In wisdom You made them all: the earth is full of Your riches. O Lord, Your glory shall endure for ever.

March 13

He teaches

"Come ye, and let us go up to the mountain of the Lord and he will teach us of his ways, and we will walk in his paths."

Isaiah 2:3

The mountain of the Lord represents His supreme love. To know about it we must go up to it. When we do, He teaches us how to live in His ways: just as He taught the Beatitudes, and the Way to heaven to the disciples on the mountain. In those days it is said the people were astonished at His doctrine. You and I will be astonished, too, if in love we listen to His teaching; and then we will know exactly how to walk in His paths.

Prayer

O Lord, instruct us and teach us in the way in which we should go: and guide us with Your eye.

March 14

Jesus comes

"For unto us a child is born, unto us a son is given."

Isaiah 9:6

These words came to the world a long, long time ago, but were not fulfilled till hundreds of years later. Yet to those people of old, and to ourselves, the message comes in the present tense. Unto us, you and me, a Child is born. Spiritual life begins inside us.

Jesus comes today, to give us a new beginning in a new birth, without which we cannot enter the kingdom of heaven. If you have knowledge of Jesus, and it is precious to you, though it be only from the innocence of your earliest memory, you will find His presence there-come to save you.

Prayer

Lord, let Your tender mercies come unto me, that I may live: for Your law is my delight.

Daily Word

March 15

His Name

"And the government shall be upon his shoulder: and his name shall be called Wonderful"

Isaiah 9:6

At first, although the Lord is with us we do not submit to His rule: so these words are in the future tense. The government shall be on His shoulder: but when? Today perhaps, or tomorrow! Actually, immediately we keep His government's laws. Till then we are rebels.

But when we accept His sovereignty everything changes. We may not as yet understand much about Him, but in our new found delight we say what we do know; we call His name Wonderful! It is the most thoroughly descriptive name our awakening experience can express.

Prayer

O Lord, open you my eyes, that I may behold wondrous things out of your law: hide not your commandments from me.

Daily Word

March 16

His Name

"And his name shall be called Wonderful, Counsellor."

Isaiah 9:6

When we yield the government of our lives to the Lord, He becomes our Counsellor. We find Him so Wonderful that we listen delightedly to His advice-His counsel. We now understand what the word means, when it says, His second name shall be called Counsellor.

As we listen to His teaching we are filled more and more with wonder: His counsel is so beautiful and attractive: it is all about loving our Maker, and loving one another, and looking for the kingdom of heaven. All summed up in the new commandment: "Little children ... love one another as I have loved you."

Prayer

O Lord, hold me with Your right hand.
Guide me with Your counsel, and
afterwards receive me in heaven.

Daily Word

March 17

His Name

"And his name shall be called, Wonderful, Counsellor, The mighty God, The everlasting Father, The Prince of Peace."

Isaiah 9:6

After accepting the Lord as our Counsellor miracles begin to happen. Our blind eyes are opened, we begin to see the Lord is the Light of the world. We find the disease of selfishness is being healed: we find new delight in loving our neighbour.

The turbulent restlessness of self-seeking goes, and we say as the disciples did "what manner of man is this that even the winds and the sea obey him". Now we call His name Mighty God, and this leads us further into love, till we realise the Child born to us, is our Everlasting Father. To know this, is to come into peace-to the Prince of Peace.

Prayer

O Lord, let my mouth be filled with Your praise all the day.

Daily Word

March 18

Providence

"O Lord, you have searched me, and known me. You know my sitting down and my uprising, you understand my thought afar off."

Psalm 139:1, 2

This Psalm is full of marvellous pictures of the Lord. It tells us clearly that He knows all about us. Perhaps most of the people we know like to feel their affairs are secret to themselves. And for this there seems to be some reason. Nothing at all however, can be hidden from the Lord. If you try to hide something from Him you will quickly know in your heart that you cannot.

The Lord searches us through and through, knows all our movements and all our thoughts however far from Him they may be. His providence covers everything: either we follow Him or He follows us.

Prayer

Search me, O God, and know my heart.

March 19

Providence

"There is not a word in my tongue, but, you, O Lord, you know it altogether. You have beset me behind and before, and laid your hand upon me."

Psalm 139:4, 5

These words tell us the truth, yet we are rarely aware that the Lord knows us so well. We soon would be though, if we learned to reflect on them. Every word in our tongue is known. The Lord is behind us and before us. We can even become conscious of His hand being laid upon us. The hand representing His power and might, that so often lifts us up out of the horrible pit, and from the miry clay of self-satisfaction. We cannot fully understand this wonderful presence and knowledge of the Lord. But it can be a part of our experience.

Prayer

O Lord, lead me in the way everlasting.

Daily Word

March 20

Providence

"If I ascend up into heaven, you are there: if I make my bed in hell, behold, you are there."

Psalm 139:8

You see, there is no getting away from God. Man cannot successfully run away from God, nor from himself. The convict in Dartmoor may have just missed the death penalty, but he still has to live with himself. And where he himself is, God confronts him: whether it be in heaven or down in hell. To make one's bed in hell, is to lie down in a confirmed state of self-love and self-indulgence. To love God first is to be in heaven: to love self first is to be in hell.

Prayer

O Lord, open to me the gates of righteousness: and lead me into them. I will praise You: for You have become my salvation.

Daily Word

March 21

Providence

"I will praise you; for I am fearfully and wonderfully made: marvellous are your works; and that my soul knows right well."

Psalm 139:14

Your body is wonderfully made! It surpasses the perfection and precision of any machine. But you who live in the body, are still more fearfully and wonderfully made.

Day by day, from the cradle to the grave God is making you; so marvellously that your mind can be in the spiritual world and, through your body, in the natural world as well. His providence provides for every moment, that you may be made, through the stages of regeneration, an angel of heaven.

Prayer

O Lord, let me ever seek You and rejoice and be glad in You; let all who love Your salvation say continually, The Lord be magnified.

Daily Word

March 22

Providence

"Your eyes did see my substance, being yet imperfect; and in Your book all my members were written to be fashioned, when as yet there was none of them."

Psalm 139:16

The Lord's eyes signify His wisdom which sees all things. Our substance at first is imperfect, without form and void. But all our parts are there in their beginnings, and in a marvellous continuance of sequences they are woven together. Fashioned into form by the hands of God, though, so far as the world could see, there was nothing. By precept upon precept, line upon line; here a little and there a little you are wrought into angel-hood.

Prayer

Hear me, O Lord; for Your loving kindness is good: turn unto me according to the multitude of Your tender mercies: and hide not Your face from Your servant.

Daily Word

March 23

Walls

"And the children of Israel went into the midst of the sea upon the dry ground: and the waters were a wall to them on their right hand, and on their left."

Exodus 14:22

The Israelites journeying to Canaan picture ourselves on our way to heaven. At the outset they had to go through the sea, which represents the flood of false things that beset us; when we determine to free ourselves from the bondage of self, and to begin a new life.

It is often frightening! But if we implore the Lord He will lead us safely through. He will clear a way through this evil flood, pushing it back to right and left, so that the false things themselves become walls delineating the boundary of our evils and falsity with heaven in the middle where the Lord dwells in us.

Prayer

O Lord, let not the water flood overflow me, neither let the deep swallow me up.

Daily Word

March 24

Walls

"Violence shall no more be heard in your land, wasting nor destruction within your borders; but you shall call your walls Salvation, and your gates Praise."

Isaiah 60:18

Your land is your character. The more you keep the commandments of love to the Lord and the neighbour, the more free from violence your character becomes. The borders of your character are the teachings of the Lord that surround your activities and secure them against evil that wastes and destroys. Your walls are Salvation, that is, they are the truth, or truths, of the Lord's Word, within which you are quite secure and safe from the evils of self-love.

Prayer

Show me Your ways, O Lord; teach me Your paths. Lead me in Your truth, and teach me: for You are the God of my salvation.

March 25

Walls

"And the building of the wall of it was of jasper: and the city was pure gold, like clear glass."

Revelation 21:18

These words are telling us of the Holy City: here in particular about the wall, which was built of jasper. The Holy City pictures heaven, or more particularly the Lord's true universal church. The walls are its boundaries.

As the church has its vision and life from the Lord's Word, the walls are the Word in its natural or literal story; within which the Lord and all the wisdom of heaven dwells. On this, the outer, side of the walls is the natural world, on the other, or inner, side is the Holy City and all it represents. Jasper stones signify precious truth.

Prayer

Hear me, O Lord; for Your loving kindness is good: turn to me according to the multitude of Your tender mercies.

Daily Word

March 26

Gates

"And he (Jacob) was afraid, and said, How dreadful is this place! this is none other but the house of God, and this is the gate of heaven."

Genesis 28:17

Jacob was on a journey. At sunset he lay down to rest, and dreaming saw a ladder that reached up to heaven, and on which angels were ascending and descending. The Lord stood above and spoke to him. It was all strange and frightening. "This," he said, "is the gate of heaven."

You too, are journeying-perhaps to heaven: if so, many memories of the Lord's Word will form a ladder reaching up to God. By it, your thoughts will ascend with the angels. To become aware of this, is to experience holy fear: and like Jacob, you will say, this is none other but the gate of heaven.

Prayer

O Lord, let my mouth be filled with Your praise.

Daily Word

March 27

Gates

"And these words, which I command you this day, shall be in your heart: And you shall write them upon the posts of your house, and on your gates."

Deuteronomy 6:6, 9

The words spoken of, are the first great commandment: the Lord is one, and is to be loved with all the heart and soul and might. Of such importance were these words that the people were told to write them on the posts of their houses, and on their gates.

Spiritually understood, one's house signifies one's mind, one's own character. The gates represent the things believed, that give entrance to heart and mind. If the commandment of love to the Lord, is written on your gates, you are happy indeed.

Prayer

O Lord, let Your tender mercies come to me, that I may live: for Your commandment is my delight.

Daily Word

March 28

Gates

"And the twelve gates were twelve pearls; every several gate was of one pearl: and the street of the city was pure gold."

Revelation 21:21

The figure twelve represents something full and complete: thus the city had twelve foundations. Gates represent knowledges of the Lord that introduce, and pearls signify their precious qualities. The street inside was pure gold, showing us that the ways of the city are the ways of golden love.

Your knowledges from the Word of Jesus are your twelve precious gates of pearl. Each picture of Him that you treasure is a precious pearl. These are your own particular gates to the Holy City.

Prayer

O Lord, open to me the gates of righteousness: I will go into them, and will praise You, for You are my salvation.

March 29

Paths

"You will show me the path of life: in your presence is fullness of joy; at your right hand there are pleasures for evermore."

Psalm 16:11

Paths! So many of them, running in many different directions, and to a thousand destinations. But the Scripture here is talking of the path of life; and the path of life is the path of love. It leads to heaven and the
Lord.

In the Bible, paths usually stand for truth, and truth leads to love; and love is life. The Lord shows us this path, and by following it we come into His presence where joy is full; and there from His love, there are pleasures for evermore.

Prayer

Hear, O Lord, when I cry with my voice: have mercy also upon me, and answer me.

March 30

Paths

"Thus says the Lord, Stand ye in the ways, and see, and ask for the old paths, where is the good way, and walk therein, and ye shall find rest for your souls."

Jeremiah 6:16

Paths are often very interesting. Perhaps you remember some of the favourite paths of childhood: through a cornfield, over cliffs by the sea, or may be, along the banks of a stream.

Perhaps you remember, too, some of the old paths of Bible stories, paths you travelled over in childhood. The path by the still waters of the twenty-third Psalm. The path through the cornfields with Jesus and His disciples and many others. These are good ways to walk in; all leading to rest for your soul.

Prayer

O Lord, make me to lie down in green pastures, and lead me beside the still waters.

Daily Word

March 31

Paths

"The voice of one crying in the wilderness, Prepare ye the way of the Lord, make his paths straight."

Luke 3:4

This was the voice of John the Baptist in the wilderness. It was clear and unmistakable, telling the people to prepare a way for the Lord.

Perhaps, sometimes, you hear a voice in the wilderness of your life calling you to prepare a way for the Lord; to make straight paths for Him. You can prepare by seeking the truth, for it is truth that makes straight paths. Truth in thought and in activity. Truth is found in the teaching of the Lord: it makes straight paths when we live as it directs.

Prayer

O Lord, so teach us to number our days, that we may apply our hearts to wisdom: and rejoice and be glad all our days.

April 1

Cities

"They wandered in the wilderness in a solitary way; they found no city to dwell in."

Psalm 107:4

A wilderness is a wild, uncultivated stretch of country. In the Bible it is often a picture of that part of one's mind where there is no spiritual cultivation. No growth of happy affections for goodness and truth, because no knowledge of the Lord. In such a state we feel lonely in our hearts, and wander in a solitary way without delight and hope.

We need a city to dwell in: a spiritual city where good affections and lively knowledge of the Lord are busy with the affairs of the Kingdom of Heaven. We need to receive the Holy City as it comes down out of heaven to earth.

Prayer

O Lord, we cry to you to be delivered out of our distress.

Daily Word

April 2

Cities

"Ye are the light of the world. A city that is set on a hill cannot be hid."

Matthew 5:14

In natural life all light and warmth comes from the sun. In spiritual life all light and warmth is from the Lord's wisdom and love, the sun of our souls. When we receive the Lord's wisdom and love it lights up and warms the world of our natural life as well. Then our mind becomes like a city of light set on a hill of love: it just cannot be hid. It is like a city, because it is crowded with a multitude of active affections and thoughts, engaged in the government of daily life. Spiritually, its laws and by-laws are from the commandments of the Lord.

Prayer

Except, O Lord, the city is kept by You, we labour in vain: have mercy upon us and guide us.

April 3

Cities

"And I John saw the holy city, new Jerusalem, coming down from God out of heaven, prepared as a bride adorned for her husband."

Revelation 21:2

The Holy City is a picture of the Lord's church: the next verse calls it a tabernacle. Not a tabernacle of bricks and mortar but of teachings of truth that lead to loving God and one another. It is prepared as a bride, because the Lord is the Bridegroom of His church. The Holy City comes down from heaven for it is of heaven not of the earth. It will come down into your life if you will open the door of love and receive it into heart and mind.

Prayer

O Lord of hosts, my soul longs, yea, even faints for the courts of the Lord: my heart and my flesh cries out for the living God.

April 4

Temple

"One thing have I desired of the Lord, that will I seek after; that I may dwell in the house of the Lord all the days of my life, to behold the beauty of the Lord, and to inquire in his temple."

Psalm 27:4

Desires arise from what we love. If you love the Lord you will want to dwell in His house to behold His beauty: you will desire to inquire of His will, in His temple.

If on the other hand, your first love is for yourself, your desires will be very different, they will then concern your own indulgences and interests.

The temple of the Lord represents heaven, the church, and the Word. For in these the Lord dwells.

Prayer

O Lord, let Your beauty be upon us: and establish You the work of our hands upon us.

Daily Word

April 5

Temple

"What sign show you to us, seeing that you do these things? Jesus answered and said to them, Destroy this temple, and in three days I will raise it up."

John 2:18, 19

The Jews wanted a sign, and Jesus gave them one; but in strange words. They did not understand them. "Destroy this temple," He said, "and in three days I will raise it up." Then the Jews said, the temple took forty-six years to build! But in the following verse we read, that Jesus was speaking of the temple of His body. His body represented Divine truth as Jesus said, "I am the truth". Divine truth is the temple of Divine love. The Jews destroyed this temple but in three days Jesus raised it again.

Prayer

My soul waits for You, Lord, more .than they that watch for the morning.

April 6

Tabernacle

"I will abide in your tabernacle for ever: I will trust in the covert of your wings."

Psalm 61:4

Would you like to dwell in the tabernacle for ever? It does not mean living in a tent or ecclesiastical building: these are only earthly receptacles, convenient for the meeting of the Lord with His people. Jesus Himself is the true tabernacle, and He tells us how to abide in Him. "If ye keep my commandments," He says, "ye shall abide in my love."

To live in His love forever, is to live in heaven in supreme happiness. To trust in the covert of His wings is to enjoy all the provision of His covering providence.

Prayer

Hear my cry, O God; attend to my prayer, when my heart is overwhelmed: lead me to the rock that is higher than I.

Daily Word

April 7

Incense

"And Aaron shall bum thereon sweet incense every morning: when he dresses the lamps, he shall bum incense upon it."

Exodus 30:7

The sweet perfume diffused by burning incense, represents the fragrance of one's affections when they arise from a heart burning with love: love for the Lord. Everything has its own emanation or atmosphere. Though our natural eyes may not be able to see it, we can often feel it very keenly: it may even help us to choose our company.

If in worship our hearts are not burning with love for the Lord, the fragrant incense is missing. The Lord, and our guardian angels will in consequence seem distant from us.

Prayer

Lord let my prayer be set fast before You as incense and the lifting up of my hands as the evening sacrifice.

Daily Word

April 8

Incense

"According to the custom of the priest's office, his (Zacharias) lot was to burn incense when he went into the temple of the Lord."

Luke 1:9

The priest's lot, was to burn incense when he went into the temple, because burning incense represented prayers and worship. Incense gives its perfume when it is burned, likewise our worship is fragrant when it burns, that is, when it is alight with love. Worship without love is lacking in spirit: it is cold and merely formal. When our hearts are alive with love the angels are near us, as indeed, one appeared to Zacharias.

Prayer

Cause me Lord, to hear Your loving kindness in the morning; for in You do I trust: cause me to know the way wherein I should walk; for I lift up my soul to You.

April 9

Incense

"And the smoke of the incense, which came with the prayers of the saints, ascended up before God out of the angel's hand."

Revelation 8:4

Spiritually, the smoke of the incense pictures the devotions of those who worship the Lord. Their prayers ascending to God out of the angel's hand, is a picture of the angels who have charge over us; who are ever ready to communicate between us and heaven.

This vision reminds us, too, of the angels Jacob saw ascending the ladder, step by step, to God Who stood at the top. When your heart burns with love it produces spiritual perfume, which in the Bible is likened to the smoke of incense.

Prayer

God be merciful to us, and bless us; and cause His face to shine upon us.

April 10

Rain

"Give ear, O ye heavens, and I will speak; and hear O earth, the words of my mouth. My doctrine shall drop as the rain, my speech shall distil as the dew, as the small rain upon the tender herb, and as the showers upon the grass."

Deuteronomy 32:1, 2

In the Bible water corresponds to truth, and rain corresponds to truth falling from the spiritual skies of the Lord's Word. When rain falls on the earth it comes together and forms pools of water: and when truth falls into our minds it forms pools of truth, which we call teaching or doctrine. Thus the words of the Lord, and His doctrine, are said to drop as the rain.

Prayer

Lord give me understanding, and I shall keep Your law; yea, I shall observe it with my whole heart.

Daily Word

April 11

Rain

"The Lord shall open unto you his good treasure, the heaven to give the rain to your land in his season, and to bless all the work of your hand."

Deuteronomy 28:12

All blessings come from the Lord, none from ourselves. He opens to us His good treasure, and out of heaven falls the rain. In the world it is natural rain, but into the land of our minds, it is spiritual rain, which is truth. The truth of His love. It comes in the changing seasons of experience to enliven all our activities by cleansing and refreshing. His doctrine falls from heaven as rain, and it always comes to bless the work of our hands.

Prayer

Let my cry come before You, O Lord: give me understanding according to your Word.

Daily Word

April 12

Rain

"But I say to you, Love your enemies... that ye may be the children of your Father which is in heaven: for he makes his sun to rise on the evil and on the good, and sends rain on the just and on the unjust."

Matthew 5:44, 45

As the Lord makes His sun shine on all, evil and good alike, so does the sun of His love shine on all without distinction. And just as the rain falls on all, so does His truth, without any difference between the just and the unjust.

The Giver never changes, neither do the gifts. All the variations of difference arise from the form of the receiver. Learn to receive the rain of truth so that it may guide your steps into the ways of peace; it will bring you inestimable blessings.

Prayer

O Lord, lead me in Your truth, and teach me: for You are the God of my salvation.

Daily Word

April 13

Wells

"And God opened her eyes, and she saw a well of water; and she went, and filled the bottle with water, and gave the lad drink."

Genesis 21:19

Ishmael was about to die of thirst. It is a picture of our understanding languishing for truth. God opening Hagar's eyes, represents the light that comes from our longing for knowledge.

When we thirst and long for truth, God shows it to us. The well of water represents God's truth in His Word. Filling a bottle is like taking enough for our immediate need. Giving the lad to drink signifies satisfying our innocent affection, with the refreshing truth of the Lord's teaching. God will open your eyes if you
ask Him.

Prayer

Hear me, O Lord; for Your loving kindness is good: turn to me according to the multitude of Your tender mercies.

Daily Word

April 14

Wells

"Therefore with joy shall ye draw water out of the wells of salvation."

Isaiah 12:3

Joy means delight: water corresponds to truth: Wells signify depths of truth; and salvation is security from evil and its consequences.

To draw water out of the wells of salvation is to draw truth out of the Lord's Word. Every little passage of the Word is a well of truth much deeper than appears from the surface. And every little drop of truth, when applied to life, saves. But the wells are deep, and only joy can draw it out. Joy comes from love; so love the Bible and its teachings, and you will soon be drawing water out of the wells of salvation.

Prayer

O Lord, unless Your law had been my delights, I should have perished in my affliction. I am thine, save me.

Daily Word

April 15

Wells

"But whoever drinks of the water that I shall give him shall never thirst; but the water that I shall give him shall be in him a well of water springing up into everlasting life."

John 4:14

When the Lord gives us the water, or truth of His Word, it forms wells in our memories; and springs up from these wells, into the love of everlasting life. The more we love the truth, the more we are able to receive from the Lord: thus our wells become deeper, and spring up with increasing delight. Whoever drinks of the water Jesus gives can never thirst. No one suffers thirst in everlasting life.

Prayer

O Lord, I stretch forth my hands to You: my soul thirsts after You, as a thirsty land. I lift up my soul to You.

April 16

Fountains

"For the Lord your God brings you into a good land, a land of brooks of water, of fountains and depths that spring out of valleys and hills."

Deuteronomy 8:7

It is indeed a good land, but the Lord can only bring us into it as we follow Him. It is a picture of the heaven-state, both as to place, when we leave the natural world, and to perception in the mind as we journey there. It is constantly refreshed by brooks of truth running through our daily activities. And fountains of truth spring up from the valleys and hills of our alternating states of love for the Lord.

Prayer

O Lord, cause me to hear Your loving kindness in the morning; for in You do I trust: cause me to know the way wherein I should walk; for I lift up my soul to You.

April 17

Fountains

"For the Lamb which is in the midst of the throne shall feed them, and shall lead them to living fountains of waters: and God shall wipe away all tears from their eyes."

Revelation 7:17

The Lord Jesus Christ, The Lamb, is right in the midst of the throne in heaven. It is He Who feeds the people of His flock and He Who leads them to the lovely fountains of living waters-the sparkling crystal truths of His love. And to crown all our happiness, He wipes away all our tears. This is what it is like to be in heaven, where all is lovely and beautiful, and where the Lamb is ever in the midst. If we wish we can begin to be in heaven even now.

Prayer

Turn us again, O God, and cause Your face to shine; and we shall be saved.

April 18

Stones

"And Joshua set up twelve stones in the midst of Jordan, in the place where the feet of the priests which bare the ark of the covenant stood: and they are there to this day."

Joshua 4:9

Joshua represents the law of the Lord combating evil, and leading to good. The number twelve represents all, or what is full and complete just as the twelve disciples figuratively represent all who follow the Lord. Stones correspond to truth, and twelve stones to all the truth of faith. The twelve tribes set their twelve stones in Jordan, as a memory of where the commandments of God, in the ark of the covenant, held back the waters for them to cross.

Prayer

Lead me O Lord, in Your righteousness because of my enemies; make Your way straight before my face.

April 19

Bones

"Make me to hear joy and gladness; that the bones which you have broken may rejoice. Hide your face from my sins, and blot out my iniquities."

Psalm 51:8, 9

Bones form the framework of the body: without them we could not stand. They correspond to basic truth which forms a foundation about which life can be built. When we become conscious of sin against the Lord it is as though His presence breaks our bones, or shows them to be not true but false supports.

But when we repent and receive His mercy, this is corrected, and we begin to build again on a foundation of truth. Then we have joy and gladness: our foundations are restored, and our bones rejoice.

Prayer

Have mercy upon me, O Lord; for I am weak: O Lord, heal me for my bones are vexed.

April 20

Bones

"Thus says the Lord God unto these bones; Behold, I will cause breath to enter into you, and ye shall live."

Ezekiel 37:5

This is from the vision of the valley of dry bones. Spiritually it is a picture of a valley of depression: of people who have little knowledge of the Lord. Bones, representing foundation faith or truth, are dry and uninteresting. They are scattered and unconnected without the sinews, and flesh of love. But God says He will cause breath to come that they may live. And they receive breath and live, an exceeding army. When the Lord breathes upon us, we too receive new life. Our bones of faith come together and love is breathed into them and we live.

Prayer

Return, O Lord, deliver my soul: O save me for Your mercies sake.

April 21

Bones

"All my bones shall say, Lord, who is like You, Delivering the poor from him that is too strong for him, yes, the poor and the needy from him that spoil him?"

Psalm 35:10

It means that every little truth that forms the framework of your faith will acknowledge the Lord as Saviour. The poor who are delivered, are the few humble qualities that seek good: that often withdraw into the inner chambers of the heart for fear of the worldly life without. These qualities are called "the poor" because they are in constant need of the Lord. They know they have no strength of their own in which they can trust.

Prayer

Let them, O Lord, be confounded and put to shame that seek after my soul: let them be turned back and brought to confusion that devise my hurt.

Daily Word

April 22

Angels

"The angel of the Lord encamps around them that fear the Lord, and delivers them. O taste and see that the Lord is good: blessed is the man that trusts in him."

Psalm 34:7, 8

Few people seem able to believe that angels are with them. Yet, it is so! No doubt the kind of life that some of us live repels angels. But they are round about those who fear the Lord: to fear, is not to be frightened of Him, but to have deep respect for what He says. It is to fear doing anything that would displease Him. In such case the angel of the Lord is camping near at hand to deliver us. I think sometimes, we can be almost conscious of the angel's presence.

Prayer

Be pleased, O Lord, to deliver me O Lord, make haste to help me.

Daily Word

April 23

Angels

"The enemy that sowed them (the tares) is the devil; the harvest is the end of the world; and the reapers are the angels."

Matthew 13:39

The devil, representing hell, interferes with us all along the way. He spoils our gardens by multitudes of pests, and he spoils the garden of our minds, by injecting spiritual pests in the form of false ideas and evil suggestions-the tares of the parable. But some day there will be a harvest; a harvest of all that is good and true, that we have managed to cultivate from the Lord's good seed. This harvest will be gathered in by the angels, for they are the Lord's reapers. The tares will then be taken from us and burned.

Prayer

O Lord, open You my lips; and my Mouth shall show forth Your praise.

April 24

Angels

"I fell down to worship before the feet of the angel which showed me these things. Then he said to me, See you do not: for I am your fellow servant, and of your brethren the prophets, and of them which keep the sayings of this book: worship God."

Revelation 22:8, 9

Men are sometimes prone to worship mistakenly. We must try to remember that God alone is Maker and the Giver of life. All good in angels and men is from God only: we may acknowledge good in others, and then glorify our Father in heaven from Whom it comes.

Angels are our fellow servants; they are of us, as the text says.

Prayer

Save us, O Lord our God, and gather us from among the heathen, to give thanks unto Your holy name, and to triumph in Your praise.

Daily Word

April 25

Enemies

"But my enemies are lively, and they are strong: and they that hate me wrongfully are multiplied."

>   Psalm 38:19

The Bible is the Book of the soul. It is the Word of God, full of spirit and life. Its history and geography are the servants of the life within. Bible "enemies" are representations of spiritual enemies. That is why war against them so often carries a ruthless picture of destruction. The love of self is our greatest enemy, and it is the parent of all our destroying indulgences. Like pests on a fruit tree they multiply continuously. Except the Lord was at hand to save us we would have no escape.

Prayer

O Lord, look upon my affliction, and forgive all my sins. Consider my enemies: for they are many, and they hate me with evil hatred.

Daily Word

April 26

Enemies

"Do not I hate them, O Lord, that hate you? and am not I grieved with those that rise up against you? I hate them with perfect hatred: I count them my enemies."

Psalm 139:21, 22

Hate is a hard word, and an unhappy one. But here it stands for utter adversity to all those feelings that are against the Lord: and of all the thoughts that rise up against Him. Perfect hatred is full and complete rejection of evil and false notions. It is an acknowledgement that they are of, and from Hell, and that they oppose all that is good and \vise. To grieve, is to feel sorrow that evil should come between us and the Lord.

Prayer

Deliver me, O Lord, from my enemies: I flee to you to hide me, lead me into the land of uprightness.

Daily Word

April 27

Goliath

"And there went out a champion out of the camp of the Philistines, named Goliath, of Gath, whose height was six cubits and a span."

1 Samuel 17:4

The Philistines represent false principles. Their champion is swollen with pride from his imagination of his own importance. Goliath, of Gath, is a picture to us all of what stupid, selfish pride can do.

Although it is actually of no importance, it seems to itself to be bigger and stronger than all others. Yet one little stone from the brook, representing, one little truth from the Lord's Word, can bring it all to the ground. But Goliath, like self-love, is very sure and very boastful.

Prayer

O my God, I trust in You: let me not be ashamed, let not my enemies triumph over me.

Daily Word

April 28

The Law

"And you shall write upon the stones all the words of this law very plainly."

Deuteronomy 27:8

These were the unhewn stones, used for the building of the altar to the Lord. They represent truth from the Word unaltered by man. It is through this truth that pure worship is performed. Moses having to write on these stones the words of the law, represents God impressing upon His people the utter necessity of His commandments: and they had to be written very plainly, that they might be easily seen and so carried out in the ordinary activities of life. The law of the Lord is perfect, and when applied to life converts the soul.

Prayer

O Lord, Your hands have made me and fashioned me: give me understanding, that I may learn Your commandments.

April 29

The Law

"The steps of a good man are ordered by the Lord: and he delights in his way. The law of his God is in his heart; none of his steps shall slide."

Psalm 37:23, 31

God is our Maker, and His laws are for our good. When we respect them our steps are ordered by Him and all is delightful.

To have God's law in our hearts is to love it. And when we love it, all our ways are directed by its regulations. Then none of our steps slide: our ways are securely guided by unchanging and eternal order. Day by day we step on, into the ways of peace.

Prayer

O Lord, order my steps in Your Word: and let not any iniquity have dominion over me. Make Your face to shine upon Your servant; and teach me Your statutes.

April 30

The Law

Jesus said, "Think not that I am come to destroy the law, or the prophets: I am not come to destroy, but to fulfil."

                              Matthew 5:17

Often, we read in the New Testament, that this or that was done to fulfil the Scriptures. In every part the Scriptures display, and teach, the laws of creation, and of life. They cannot be destroyed, they are the foundations on which the whole of life is founded.

When we neglect these Divine laws our only hope is Jesus; He comes to us to restore order into our lives, not by destroying the law, but by enabling us to fulfil its requirements.

Thus we come again into harmony with heaven and into the ways of peace.

Prayer

O Lord, let Your tender mercies come to me, that I may live: for Your law is my delight.

May 1

Beauty

"One thing have I desired of the Lord, that will I seek after; that I may dwell in the house of the Lord all the days of my life, to behold the beauty of the Lord, and to inquire in his temple."

Psalm 27:4

Just one thing to desire of the Lord, and one thing to seek: to dwell in His house, and to behold His beauty, in all the changing states of life. What a vision of delight! The security of His house, and the beauty of His love and wisdom. We think of the Lord in many different ways: but do we think of His beauty? Do you? All beauty is from good, and the Lord is Goodness itself.

Prayer

O Lord, let Your beauty be upon us: and establish You the work of our hands upon us.

Daily Word

May 2

Beauty

"Let your work appear to your servants, and your glory to their children. And let the beauty of the Lord our God be upon us."

Psalm 90:16, 17

The Lord's great work is to save us from ourselves. As we follow Him, He leads us in the paths of righteousness, away from the destroying sins of self-indulgence. When we come to see His goodness following us, and the wonder of His work in guiding, we gladly acknowledge His glory. All the delight that comes into our changing life we see to come from Him. It is all His beauty falling upon us; and to taste it, is to long for more.

Prayer

O Lord, revive us again: show us Your mercy, and grant us Your salvation.

Daily Word

May 3

Beauty

"Awake, Awake; put on your strength, O Zion; put on your beautiful garments, O Jerusalem, the holy city."

Isaiah 52:1

Jerusalem, the holy city, is a picture of the Lord's church; both in general and in particular. You may be a holy city yourself. You are, in so far as you acknowledge the Lord, and live from him. To awake is to be aware of the presence of the Lord. Your strength is the love He gives you. Your beautiful garments are His teachings, for they clothe your soul just as worldly garments clothe your body. If you are wise, you will put on these beautiful, warm, and comforting garments.

Prayer

Teach me Your way O Lord; and I will walk in Your truth, and glorify Your name for evermore.

Daily Word

May 4

Garments

"You cover Yourself with light as with a garment, you stretch out the heavens like a curtain.

Psalm 104:2

The Lord is life, and life is the light of men. The Lord is clothed with light, it is His garment. It is the Divine truth, pictured in the Bible, as raiment as white as light. It is white because it is innocent; and it is as the light, because where there is truth there is no darkness. The heavens are stretched out like a curtain for they are within the veil of truth.

As you receive truth from the Lord, you too in a finite way are clothed with garments of light.

Prayer

Withhold not You Your tender mercies from me, O Lord: let Your loving kindness and Your truth continually preserve me.

Daily Word

May 5

Garments

"I will greatly rejoice in the Lord, my soul shall be joyful in my God; for He has clothed me with the garments of salvation."

Isaiah 61:10

The garments of salvation! What are they? In this world's life clothes are for the body, but in spiritual life garments clothe the soul. Spiritual garments are composed of the teachings of the Lord that clothe, or surround our love for Him.

It is the truth of these teachings, that saves us from the devastating evils of self-love. To be clothed in these garments is something to rejoice, and be joyful about. They are indeed the garments of salvation, and God's gift to those who love Him.

Prayer

In You, O Lord, do I put my trust: let me never be put to confusion. Deliver me in Your righteousness and save me.

May 6

Garments

"And it came to pass, as they were much perplexed thereabout, behold, two men stood by them in shining garments."

Luke 24:4

Two men from heaven, for they were angels. In shining garments; for folk in heaven are clothed in garments that are effulgent with light, from love in their hearts. These two angels were ministering in the sepulchre of Jesus. Sometimes we wonder about heaven, and those who are there: are they anything like us? What kind of clothes do they wear? The disciples saw these angels as men, and they saw their shining garments, and heard them talking. They were real!

Prayer

Not to us, O Lord, not to us but to Your Name give glory, for Your mercy, and for Your truth's sake.

May 7

Fire

"Then the fire of the Lord fell, and consumed the burnt sacrifice, and the wood, and the stones, and the dust, and licked up the water that was in the trench."

1 Kings 18:38

Elijah built the altar, then had water poured on the burnt offering and wood, till it overflowed and filled the surrounding trench. Then calling on the Lord, fire came down and burned the sacrifice and wood, the stones and dust, and water in the trench.

It pictures the fire of God's love falling into all worship that is offered in humility to Him. This love enters into everything, from greatest to least, and so affects the water (truth) that love and truth become closely conjoined: till we cannot tell one from the other.

Prayer

O Lord, open You my lips; and my mouth shall show forth Your praise.

May 8

Fire

"He answered and said, Behold, I see four men loose, walking in the midst of the fire, and they have no hurt; and the form of the fourth is like the Son of God."

Daniel 3:25

In the Bible, fire corresponds to love: sometimes representing love in an evil sense, sometimes in a good sense.
Nebuchadnezzar full of fury with Shadrach, Meshach and Abednego, cast them into a burning fiery furnace. Then sat down to watch the flames destroy them. But the fire did not destroy them. You see, the fire here, represented evil love, and it could not hurt men who trusted God. When you feel the burning of evil love about you, look to the Lord: He will send His angels to save you.

Prayer

O keep my soul, Lord, and deliver me: for I put my trust in You.

May 9

Fire

"John answered, saying to them all, I indeed baptise you with water; but one mightier than I comes, the latch of whose shoes I am not worthy to touch: he shall baptise you with the Holy Ghost and with fire."

Luke 3:16

We are introduced into the life of religion, through the story of the Bible. Afterwards a great experience awaits us. It is the coming of Jesus, to baptise us with the Holy Spirit, and the fire of His divine love. The Holy Spirit is the divine truth inside the letter of the Word. Fire is the goodness of His mighty love, that is, the very life of the Word.

Prayer

Let Your mercies come also unto me, O Lord, even Your salvation, according to Your word: for I trust in Your word.

May 10

Foundation

"If the foundations be destroyed, what can the righteous do?"

Psalm 11:3

Once, I built a wall! five feet high and fifteen inches wide, all of stones. I was quite proud of it, and so was the family. A few weeks later we had a period of heavy rain and my grand wall fell down. It was very sad: but a splendid lesson, for I had forgotten the foundations. Without foundations what can the righteous do? Floods of adversity come and we tumble. But truly wonderful foundations and stones are available: they are the teachings of the Lord. Especially the two great commandments of love to God and love to the neighbour. Nothing can destroy these.

Prayer

I entreated Your favour, O Lord, with my whole heart: O teach me Your ways, and turn my feet unto Your testimonies.

Daily Word

May 11

Foundations

"Of old have You laid the foundation of the earth: and the heavens are the work of Your hands."

Psalm 102:25

Remember, God created the heavens first, and then the earth. The foundations of the earth are people in whom heaven rests. Jesus tells us to seek heaven first. If you seek heaven, by giving it first place in your life, your outer life representing the earth, will be its foundation. Below your life, are the outer and lowest truths of all, forming the boundaries of creation. Heaven is the Lord's throne, the earth is His footstool. The better the foundations your earth life provides, the more of heaven you will receive.

Prayer

O Lord, open to me the gates of righteousness, that I may go in and praise the Lord, for You are become my salvation.

Daily Word

May 12

Foundations

"And the wall of the city had twelve foundations, and in them the names of the twelve apostles of the Lamb."

Revelation 21:14

The holy city, representing the Lord's church, comes down from heaven and enters into us as we receive it. The wall of the city represents the teachings of the Word. These surround the spirit and life within. Walls have foundations, and these of the holy city are the eternal truths of the Lord's love. They are said to have in them the names of the twelve apostles, because the number twelve represents what is complete, and the apostles stand for all who follow Jesus. The Lamb is the Lord.

Prayer

O God, be merciful unto us, and bless us; and cause Your face to shine upon us.

Daily Word

May 13

Songs

"And he has put a new song in my mouth, even praise to our God: many shall see it, and fear, and shall trust in the Lord."

Psalm 40:3

Gladness in the heart tends to cause singing. You of course, have noticed this in your own experience. This passage is a picture of one who has been lifted up by the Lord, out of a horrible pit, and from miry clay.

The pit and mire represent the degradation and tenacity of the evils of self-love. To be lifted up, and saved from them, is indeed to find a new gladness, and a new song of praise to the Lord. When others see this, they are filled with wonder, and themselves begin to trust the Lord.

Prayer

O Lord, let all those that seek you, rejoice and be glad in you.

Daily Word

May 14

Songs

"They that carried us away captive required of us a song; and they that wasted us required of us mirth, saying, sing us one of the songs of Zion. How shall we sing the Lord's song in a strange land?"

Psalm 137:3, 4

These poor people were prisoners in Babylon! They are a picture of ourselves; when the sins of self-will have captivated and wasted our strength. Once we were happy, but now have come into the far country of want and desolation. Songs and mirth (Joy) have departed! We want to be happy but how can we sing the Lord's song in this strange land? The songs of Zion are for those who are happy in the Lord.

Prayer

Lord, let my prayer be set forth before You as incense; and the lifting up of my hands as the evening sacrifice.

Daily Word

May 15

Noise and Singing

"Make a joyful noise unto the Lord, all you lands. Serve the Lord with gladness: come before His presence with singing."

Psalm 100:1, 2

How many of us who cannot sing, rejoice in making a joyful noise? When the heart is full of gladness, something must happen. We serve the Lord with gladness, when we find delight in living from His teachings, and commandments. It is this kind of life that makes a joyful noise, for in it all the affections of the heart sing in the presence of the Lord. You see, He is present where He is loved, and where He
is loved, His commandments are kept.

Prayer

Create in me a clean heart, O God; and renew a right spirit within me. O Lord open You my lips; and my mouth shall show forth Your praise.

Daily Word

May 16

Fear

"The fear of the Lord is the beginning of wisdom: a good understanding have all they that do his commandments: his praise endures for ever."

Psalm 111:10

Fear! a word used in a variety of ways, and with many meanings. We may fear consequences arising from something we have done; the wild nature of a storm, or an impending operation: or the approach to a distinguished person.

On the other hand we may be filled with holy fear lest we offend the Lord, or stray from His leading. The fear of the Lord is the beginning of wisdom, because it implies deep respect for His commandments which, when followed, bring us into a wise and happy life. But at last perfect love casts out all fear.

Prayer

Lord, open You my eyes, that I may behold wondrous things out of Your law.

Daily Word

May 17

Fear

"Then they that feared the Lord spake often one to another, and the Lord hearkened, and heard it, and a book of remembrance was written before him for them that feared the Lord, and that thought upon his name."

Malachi 3:16

This is the fear of deep respect: of reverent humility. Those who experience it delight to talk together of the Lord. As the Lord, from His infinite wisdom, knows the least thoughts of our hearts, He is said to have hearkened to our words.

The book of remembrance is a picture of our interior memory, in which everything we have done and experienced is recorded: it is our book of life. This book is written before the Lord, for He sees and knows all things.

Prayer

In You, O Lord, do I put my trust; let me never be ashamed: deliver me in Your righteousness.

Daily Word

May 18

Fear

"Fear not; for I am with you: be not dismayed: for I am your God: I will strengthen you; yea, I will help you; yea, I will uphold you with the right hand of my righteousness."

Isaiah 41:10

Do you sometimes feel lonely and dismayed? Or frail and helpless? Well, cheer up! The Lord is with you! In your weakness He will be your strength. Though you cannot face life's problems alone, with His help you can. Learn to walk with Him, and you will come to feel His strong hand holding yours; and leading you into the paths of righteousness. Fear not, be strong and of a good courage.

Prayer

Hear, O Lord, and have mercy upon me: Lord, be You my helper. You have turned for me my mourning into dancing, and girded me with gladness.

May 19

Courage

"Be strong and of good courage, fear not, nor be afraid of them: for the Lord your God, He it is that does go with you; he will not fail you, nor forsake you."

Deuteronomy 31:6

We too, like the children of Israel, are journeying to the Promised Land. Like them, we often find the going difficult and sometimes quite frightening. We easily forget that although we may be "grown up" we are still children and need our Father's strength and care.

But we can be strong and of a good courage, if we remember that the Lord our God goes with us. His good love holds us in His care, and His wonderful unchanging truth protects us continuously. He will not fail us!

Prayer

Deliver me, O Lord, from my enemies: I flee to You to hide me.

Daily Word

May 20

Courage

"Wait on the Lord; be of good courage, and he shall strengthen your heart: wait, I say, on the Lord."

Psalm 27:14

To wait on the Lord is patiently to trust Him. To be of good courage is to walk fearlessly with Him. To be strengthened in heart is to feel His loving care. These are the things that make all the difference. They are qualities that can be yours too, for God's gifts are for us all. But even God does not give us things when we refuse to receive them. His part is to give, ours to receive. In order to receive, we must seek His face, and listen to His word, and thus wait patiently for Him.

Prayer

Teach me Your way, O Lord, and lead me in a plain path, because of my enemies.

Daily Word

May 21

Gentleness

"Your right hand has held me up, and your gentleness has made me great."

Psalm 18:35

The Lord's right hand is a picture of His loving truth. It ever holds us up. It is greater than all our difficulties: and equal to all our needs. And His gentleness makes us great because it is good. And how very wonderful it is to be able to receive this goodness from Him. As we learn of Him, He gives us rest, for He has told us, He is meek and lowly in heart. And in meekness, is kindliness and gentleness-true qualities, of true greatness. Truly the Lord's yoke is easy, and His burden light.

Prayer

O Lord, keep Your servant from presumptuous sins: let them not have dominion over me, then shall I be innocent from the great transgression.

Daily Word

May 22

Talking

"And these words, which I command you this day, shall be in your heart: and you shall teach them diligently to your children, and shall talk of them when you sit in your house."

Deuteronomy 6:6, 7

The words spoken of are the commandments of the Lord. They are to be in our hearts, that is, to be loved. They are to be taught diligently to our children. And we are to talk of them when sitting in the house.

Spiritually understood, one's house is one's mind; and one's children are all the little thoughts and affections that fill the mind. Talking of them is thinking, meditating and reflecting-about the Lord's commandments.

Prayer

O Lord, unless Your law had been my delights, I should have perished in my affliction. I am Yours, save me; for I have sought Your precepts.

Daily Word

May 23

Talking

"My lips shall greatly rejoice when I sing to you; and my soul, which you have redeemed. My tongue also shall talk of your righteousness all the day long."

Psalm 71:23, 24

When our worship of the Lord is humble and sincere we are filled with rejoicing. In such a state we love to talk of the Lord; and talking is often very useful, and very instructive. Without it and the communion it gives us with one another, we would suffer severe loss. To talk of the Lord with our friends can be delightful indeed. But we can only talk of His righteousness "all the day long", while we are in a state of love to Him.

Prayer

O Lord, help me to hope continually, and I will praise You more and more, then my mouth shall show forth Your righteousness.

Daily Word

May 24

Talking

"Hereafter I will not talk much with you: for the prince of this world comes, and has nothing in me."

John 14:30

Jesus had talked to the disciples and the people continually; in their synagogues and homes and by the wayside. But now He says, "I will not talk much with you." Why not? It is because of the coming of this world's prince, meaning the prince of evil. Jesus and evil have nothing in common. In so far as the devil is first with us, Jesus cannot talk much with us. Even though He did, we would not listen.

Prayer

O Lord, truly I am Your servant: You have loosed my bonds. I will offer to You the sacrifice of thanks- giving, and will call upon the name of the Lord.

May 25

Sin

"Wash me thoroughly from my iniquity, and cleanse me from my sin. For I acknowledge my transgressions: and my sin is ever before me."

Psalm 51:2, 3

Unless we washed, we would soon become unclean, and unhealthy. But we sometimes fail to realise that just as the body needs washing, so does the spirit that lives in the body: and, if not washed, it too becomes unclean, and quite unhealthy. In this passage from the Word we acknowledge our faults, and pray to the Lord to wash us clean. Then His truth, which is spiritual water, becomes active in our minds, cleanses us from sin, and produces a healthy spirit.

Prayer

O Lord, hide Your face from my sins, and blot out all my iniquities. Create in me a clean heart, O God; and renew a right spirit within me.

Daily Word

May 26

Sin

"They that are whole need not a physician; but they that are sick. I came not to call the righteous, but sinners to repentance.

Luke 5:31, 32

Here is cheering news for you and me! Jesus came as a physician to call sinners to repentance. He can heal spiritual sickness! Repentance is the prescription, but while we imagine we are righteous we don't appreciate the medicine: thus the saying of Jesus, I came not to call the righteous. Repentance, means, seeing sins to be against God, and in this acknowledgement turning from them, and abhoring them. Repentance is the Physician's medicine and it saves us from destroying sickness and disease.

Prayer

Create in me a clean heart, O God; and renew a right spirit within me. Restore to me the joy of Your salvation; and uphold me with Your free spirit.

Daily Word

May 27

Trouble

"God is our refuge and strength, a very present help in trouble."

Psalm 46:1

To love God is to be conjoined to Him. The more closely we are conjoined, the happier we become. And in this happiness we find a secure and wonderful refuge: no evil can hurt us here. God is also our strength when we love Him: and He has all power in heaven and in earth; He is stronger than all the spiritual enemies that beset us, He can defend us fully in any circumstances. And He is indeed a very present help in trouble.
Tell Him your trouble, lay it all out before Him in detail: then you will know from experience, that He is in truth your refuge, and your strength.

Prayer

Be merciful to me, O God, for my soul trusts in You.

Daily Word

May 28

Trouble

"The sorrows of death compassed me, and the pains of hell has hold upon me: I found trouble and sorrow. Then called I upon the name of the Lord."

Psalm 116:3, 4

Many of us forget the Lord. Then, when troubles come, and we are worried and distressed, we remember Him again: this is one of the blessings of adversity. The sorrows of death arise from self-love, which always kills happiness. The pains of hell are the miseries of retribution, for all sins hit back: there are no exceptions! The result is trouble and sorrow. But trouble and sorrow brought the prodigal to himself, and turned him home again. They can lead us also to remember the Lord.

Prayer

O Lord, I am poor and needy, and my heart is wounded within me. O save me according to Your mercy.

May 29

Washing

"I will wash my hands in innocence: so will I compass your altar, O Lord."

Psalm 26:6

Our hands do most of our work, they represent our daily activities. To wash them, is to cleanse our ways, and to do so in innocence, is to wash them in the Lord's teachings which are truth. In so far as we live from self we are guilty, but in so far as we act from the Lord we are innocent. To compass the altar of the Lord is to draw near to Him. It is to ascend into the hill of the Lord, which those do who have clean hands and a pure heart.

Prayer

O Lord, with my whole heart have I sought You: O let me not wander from Your commandments. Your word have I hid in my heart.

May 30

Washing

"Wash you, make you clean; put away the evil of your doings from before my eyes; cease to do evil."

Isaiah 1:16

When you wash your hands, say to yourself, "I must wash my spiritual hands as well." Then, you will begin to see why: and to understand what spiritual washing means. For this you will need Bible water which is God's truth. This will wash you and make you really clean. It will remove evil from your doings through your desisting from them; and in looking on you, the Lord will see before His eyes, someone who loves Him. While washing, reflect on the evils you are imploring Him to remove, and soon they will cease to afflict you.

Prayer

O Lord, send out Your light and Your truth: let them lead me; let them bring me to Your holy hill, and to Your tabernacle.

Daily Word

May 31

Washing

"And he said to me, These are they which came out of great tribulation, and have washed their robes, and made them white in the blood of the Lamb."

Revelation 7:14

Tribulation is a part of the cost of regeneration. At the time it seems a heavy cost, but when it is all behind us we forget the trial: how can we do otherwise? We are home, and all is lovely.

We know what white robes mean, for the Bible tells us; the fine white linen is the righteous acts of the saints. We make our robes white by making our actions clean: by washing them in the blood of the Lamb-in the Lord's divine truth.

Prayer

Lord, give me understanding and I shall keep Your law; yea, I shall observe it with my whole heart.

Daily Word

June 1

Bed

"For the bed is shorter than that a man can stretch himself on it: and the covering narrower than that he can wrap himself in it."

Isaiah 28:20

A strange passage, how can it be of use to us? Well, the bed is a picture of the teaching of the Lord that forms our faith. As we rest the body in bed so we rest the soul in our faith. If our faith is too short to stretch in, it is short of love: love expands, and lengthens our bed of faith.

The covering pictures the truth, or truths of our doctrine, with which we wrap ourselves up. If these are cold for the want of love, they will be too narrow to cover us.

Prayer

Help me O Lord my God: O save me according to Your mercy.

June 2

Bed

"He that made me whole, the same said to me, Take up your bed, and walk."

John 5:11

Most of us spend a third of our life in bed. Think of it! One year out of every three you have probably spent in bed. The sick man at Bethesda had been in bed much longer. It was time to get up and make some effort. But his bed, representing Faith, needed Jesus. No one else could help him. "Rise," said Jesus, "take up your bed and walk." He did! It is a lesson to us all.

Directly we take up our Faith, because the Lord tells us to, we are healed, and carry our bed, which means we live our Faith, and walk into Life itself-for we are now living with Jesus, our God.

Prayer

Be merciful to me, O God, for my soul trusts in You.

Daily Word

June 3

Praying

"As for me, I will call upon God; and the Lord shall save me. Evening and morning, and at noon, will I pray, and cry aloud: and he shall hear my voice."

Psalm 55:16, 17

Is this you speaking? Are you calling upon God? If so He will save you; but from what? There is one thing to be saved from: sin, and its destroying tentacles. To call on God is to look towards Him: away from self.

Evening, when the sun goes down, is a picture of our spiritual state when love seems to be departing. Morning represents a new beginning with love rising again, and noon the fullness of love. To pray and cry aloud is to long ardently for the Lord.

Prayer

O Lord, let my prayer come before You: incline Your ear to my cry.

June 4

Praying

"All things, whatsoever ye shall ask in prayer, believing, ye shall receive."

Matthew 21:22

Have you tried praying like this? If so perhaps you have been disappointed. Yet many have found these words of Jesus wonderfully true. The word "believing" is the word that makes the difference. It is the affirmative attitude that brings the object of desire near to us. When we pray to the Lord we must believe in Him, which means, love and trust Him. Then we shall only ask for those things that are in harmony with His will, and He will certainly give them to us. Even to the removal of mountains of selfishness.

Prayer

Hear my cry, O God; attend to my prayer. From the end of the earth will I cry to You, when my heart is overwhelmed: lead me to the rock that is higher than I.

Daily Word

June 5

Seeking

"Seek ye first the Kingdom of God and his righteousness."

Matthew 6:33

Most of us are life-long seekers. Perhaps the big difference between folk arises from what they seek. Jesus tells us to seek the Kingdom of God, and He puts it first. That is first in importance. But He does not tell us where to seek it, not exactly anyhow. Where do we seek for it? We can seek knowledge of it in His Word. We can make it the first thing to seek in one another, in our homes, and always in our work and social life. God hides His Kingdom within us, and tells us to look for it. It is a most important task.

Prayer

O God, you are my God, early will I seek You, my soul thirsts for You.

June 6

Seeking

"When you said, Seek ye my face; my heart said to You, Your face, Lord, will I seek."

Psalm 27:8

When our hearts purpose to do as the Lord says, we are on our way to heaven. Jesus tells us that if we seek we shall find. To seek His face is to seek life itself. It is to seek the sun of love. The face of the Lord is the countenance of Divine love and wisdom.
It is said we become like what we seek. The miser seeks money and becomes a picture of cold cringing avarice. He who always seeks the face of the Lord, at last becomes an image and likeness of His Maker.

Prayer

Hear, O Lord, when I cry with my voice: have mercy also upon me, and answer me.

Daily Word

June 7

Idleness

"Why stand ye here all the day idle?"

Matthew 20:6

Idleness is the devil's pillow. In its bed is disease and death. We are born to be useful, and in service to one another to find happiness and delight. Nothing in the order of God's creation is idle. All things from least to greatest serve the common good.

It is the same in the body, if the blood ceased to flow the body would die. Each organ, and each part, must be active in service to all other parts. Health will not tolerate idleness. As with the body so with the soul: every part must perform a use to the whole. We, and all within us, must work in the Lord's vineyard.

Prayer

Consider and hear me, O Lord my God: lighten my eyes, lest I sleep the sleep of death.

June 8

Space

"And the servant said, Lord, it is done as you have commanded, and yet there is room."

Luke 14:22

Space is strange!
There was a man who wanted to die before heaven was full, while there was space or room for him. He did not know that to live in heaven is to live in love - God's love. "If ye keep my commandments ye shall abide in my love," said Jesus. To abide in His love is to live in heaven.

There is so much spiritual space in God's love that there is always room. It is infinite! All who wisely love His commandments, however different they may be; will find a home there.

Prayer

Teach me to do Your will, O Lord, for You are my God: Your spirit is good, lead me into the land of uprightness.

Daily Word

June 9

Bondage

"I am the Lord your God, which have brought you out of the land of Egypt, out of the house of bondage."

Exodus 20:2

In this verse Egypt stands for our natural life, and its delight in science and knowledge. And the house of bondage represents our captivity. How easily we become absorbed in natural things, giving to them
our health, and the best of our days.
But the position should be reversed: spiritual life should control natural life, for the end of all our endeavour must be the Kingdom of God. How can we shake ourselves from the dust and be free? Only by remembering the Lord our God. He alone can break our chains and lead us home.

Prayer

Keep me, O Lord, for Your name's sake: for Your righteousness' sake bring my soul out of trouble.

Daily Word

June 10

Commandments

"You shall not take the name of the Lord your God in vain."

Exodus 20:7

To think of God, and to speak of Him, without any respect, is to take His name in vain. And especially is it so, when we use His name without serious purpose and become profaners.

To use God's name vainly, cuts us off from Him, and the wonderful things He teaches. In this we cannot be guiltless, for it is an active attitude of the "self" that we love and follow: the "self" that is profane, and becomes increasingly miserable. This commandment is for our good, if we follow its lead we shall avoid much sorrow.

Prayer

Help us, O God of our salvation, for the glory of Your name; and deliver us, and purge away our sins, for Your name's sake

Daily Word

June 11

Commandments

"Remember the sabbath day, to keep it holy."

Exodus 20:8

We call the sabbath, Sunday, the day of rest. Many of us love it very much, because it has meant, and does mean, such a lot to us. But many, in these days, know it only as a holiday.

The commandments tell us to remember to keep it holy. In the ordinary sense it means that six days are for work and our own concerns, and the seventh for the Lord and His church. In a deeper sense the Sabbath represents the rest and peace the Lord brings us into through the struggles of regeneration. Thus it is a picture of heaven, and the Lord's love for us, and is indeed holy.

Prayer

Turn us again, O Lord God of hosts, cause Your face to shine; and we shall be saved.

June 12

Commandments

"Honour your father and your mother."

Exodus 20:12

In the natural sense this commandment tells us to honour our earthly parents. This, most of us do in any case, though often from reasons of relationship alone.

Spiritually, father stands for the Lord, and mother for the church. The Lord and the church are our spiritual parents. All our life is from the Lord, and the church in its true state, nourishes and cares for us as a mother. These are the father and mother we are spiritually commanded to honour. To keep this commandment, means that we enter into continuing love for the Lord and His church, ever becoming more closely conjoined.

Prayer

O Lord, truly I am Your servant; I am Your servant, and the son of Your handmaid: You have loosed my bonds.

June, 13

Commandments

"You shall not kill."

Exodus 20:13

This command in its ordinary sense is clear to all. We know that it is wrong to kill. But of course, there is always a deeper meaning, for the Bible is dealing with spiritual matters.

We are not to kill, nor try to kill, our neighbour's love for the Lord; nor his affection for others. Nor his good name and reputation. We are not to destroy anything that is good or true. Nor are we to kill by bringing into disrepute the services and teachings of the church of the Lord; nor of His Word, either in the Old or New Testaments. Anything held to be holy by others is to be respected.

Prayer

O Lord, Your hands have made me and fashioned me: give me understanding, that I may learn Your commandments.

Daily Word

June 14

Commandments

"You shall not commit adultery."

Exodus 20:14

How much happier our country would be, if this law were observed. Where it is neglected degrading conditions and misery abound; and countless children become homeless.

But this commandment also carries a deeper meaning, for within it is spiritual and refers to the spirit of mankind. To commit adultery on the spiritual plane, is to embrace adulterous feelings and thoughts. It is to attempt to mix evil with good, and false reasoning with the truths of the Lord. When this is done the soul sickens and falls into decay. To try to break the Lord's commandments is to commit adultery, for they are good, and to pervert them with evil is bad.

Prayer

Hear me speedily, O Lord: my spirit fails: hide not Your face from me, lest I be like them that go down into the pit.

Daily Word

June 15

Commandments

"You shall not steal."

> Exodus 20:15

There are those who steal with deliberate purpose. They are universally despised: and they are a public menace. There are others who would not dream of snatching a handbag, and yet they will pilfer where they see plenty. And again there are those who would not steal money, and yet will gladly steal their employer's time, and take wages for work not done. Sin is strangely subtle. But every self-imposed restraint is good.

Then, there is spiritual stealing. Taking credit for good that comes only from the Lord. Stealing our neighbour's good name, and taking knowledge from the Bible, solely for our own ends and reputation.

Prayer

Set a watch, O Lord, before my mouth; keep the door of my lips. Incline not my heart to any evil thing.

Daily Word

June 16

Commandments

"You shall not bear false witness against your neighbour."

Exodus 20:16

How easy it sometimes is, to disregard this commandment. And what a lot of sadness arises from our carelessness. False witness! What a nasty thing it is! It may be only a gesture or just a passive attitude. Then again it may be a positive statement quite unjustified by the actual position. Indeed, it is any act or word that gives a false picture of someone's character. It i against our neighbour, and so against God. Spiritually, it is denial of God's love, and God's wisdom, either by thought, or word, or attitude.

Prayer

O Lord, show Your marvellous loving kindness, You that saves by Your right hand them that put their trust in You from those that rise up against them.

June 17

Commandments

"You shall not covet ... anything that is your neighbour's."

Exodus 20:17

To covet, is to eagerly want what is another's for oneself. If we did not love ourselves we would never covet another's goods. It is evidence of selfishness, and of discontent. It is to put self first.

A deeper spiritual meaning is, that we must not covet the self-loving way of life. We must not want to move away from the Lord's ways, to lust after the things His commandments forbid. Neither should we covet the good and happiness of our neighbour for ourselves. Our neighbour's good in every respect is to be respected even as our own.

Prayer

O Lord, make me go in the path of Your commandments; for therein do I delight. Incline my heart to Your testimonies, and not to covetousness.

Daily Word

June 18

Animals

"And God made the beast of the earth after his kind, and cattle after their kind, and every thing that creeps upon the earth after his kind."

Genesis 1:25

Beasts, cattle and creeping things, have a spiritual significance as well as a natural place on the earth. In the Bible where spiritual values are of first importance they correspond to your affections.

The earth where the animals live represents your external life: it is crowded with affections of every kind. Some of them noble, some inferior, and others that as it were, creep about among your lowest appetites. When you read of these things in the Word, try to see their place in the cosmos that is you.

Prayer

O Lord, so foolish was I, and ignorant: I was as a beast before You.

Daily Word

June 19

Horses

"An horse is a vain thing for safety: neither shall he deliver any by his great strength."

Psalm 33:17

In general, in a natural way, a horse signifies intelligence. Spiritually, the horse in the Bible signifies one's affection for knowledge or understanding. Sometimes a good affection is represented, at others a merely selfish one.

When the picture is one of trust in one's self-derived intelligence, then one's horse is a vain thing for safety. Although we may be very self-confident in our own understanding of a matter our strength is vain it cannot save us. The eye of the Lord is upon them that fear Him (verse 18).

Prayer

O Lord, let not the foot of pride come against me, and let not the hand of the wicked remove me.

Daily Word

June 20

Horses

"And I saw, and behold a white horse: and He that sat on him had a bow: and a crown was given to Him: and he went forth conquering, and to conquer."

Revelation 6:2

A white horse signifies the understanding of Bible truth, for white signifies truth and a horse intelligence. The bow signifies the teaching of truth, and a crown the sovereignty of love. And going forth conquering, and to conquer, represents the supremacy of love through the truth of the Word.

All this, and much more, John saw when his spirit-eyes were opened. You may not see as John did, nevertheless you will come to see wonderful things if you read your Bible in the presence of the Lord.

Prayer

Show me Your ways, O Lord; teach me Your paths, for You are the God of my salvation.

Daily Word

June 21

The Ass

"And Balaam rose up in the morning, and saddled his donkey, and went with the princes of Moab."

Numbers 22:21

Balaam is a picture of those, who with their lips, acknowledge the Lord, yet in heart are far from Him. They are ever ready to compromise with the enemy of the church. To rise up in the morning represents the beginning of a new state. To saddle his donkey, signifies to reason with himself in preparation for his journey with the princes of Moab: the princes are the enemy's messengers. The donkey represents natural reasoning which carries man's lower desires. Like the donkey, natural reasoning can be slow, and stubborn.

Prayer

Examine me, O Lord, and prove me; try my reins and my heart. Gather not my soul with sinners, in whose hands is mischief.

Daily Word

June 22

The Ass

"And Jesus, when he had found a young donkey, sat thereon; as it is written, Fear not, daughter of Sion: behold, your King comes, sitting on an donkey's colt."

John 12:14, 15

Jesus riding on an ass is expressive of regal authority, for in olden times it was often the custom of kings. But in the Bible words carry fuller, deeper meanings. The donkey represents man's lower intelligence or natural reasoning; for as the donkey carries the body, so natural reason carries one's mind. The king coming, sitting on an donkey's colt, represents the Lord's triumph in bringing all things of His natural humanity under the submissive control of His divine love.

Prayer

O Lord God of my salvation, I have cried day and night before You. Let my prayer come before You: incline Your ear unto my cry.

Daily Word

June 23

Sheep

"Rejoice with me; for I have found my sheep which was lost."

Luke 15:6

Sheep are among the gentle animals. In the Bible they usually represent those who are in that which is good. In this parable the man who found his sheep, represents the Lord. The sheep might be you or me.
Or it might be something good you or I had lost. The Lord is the Good Shepherd Who gives His life-Himself-continuously for good, and to seek and save it when it goes astray. The Lord is happy when a lost sheep is found, and calls all who love Him together, to rejoice with Him.

Prayer

Hear my prayer, O Lord, and let my cry come unto You. Hide not Your face from me in the day when I am in trouble.

June 24

Birds

Jesus says ... "The foxes have holes, and the birds of the air have nests; but the Son of man has nowhere to lay his head."

Matthew 8:20

Foxes represent the kind of prudence that hides in the ground of self-love. The birds of the air represent our thoughts that flit about in every direction. These have their nests, or dwellings, in our affections. But often there is no place where the Lord can find cover, or a resting place in our minds. By the Son of man the Lord is represented as to His Word, in which He is revealed to us as Man. Spiritually understood birds are thoughts of all kinds.

Prayer

O Lord, wash me thoroughly from my iniquity, and cleanse me from my sin. For I acknowledge my transgressions: and my sin is ever before me.

Daily Word

June 25

Doves

"And I said, Oh that I had wings like a dove! for then would I fly away, and be at rest."

Psalm 55:6

Doves are delightful! They do not destroy other birds nor their nests: they are birds of peace. In the Word they correspond to what is good, and to truth. As their wings lift them up towards the sky, so does the truth of what is good lift us up towards the skies of heaven.

To long for wings like a dove is to earnestly desire the truths of peace and goodness. To fly away, is to be able to lift ourselves above the clamour of selfish life, and so find rest.

Prayer

O Lord, hasten my escape from the windy storm and tempest. Evening, and morning, and at noon will I pray, and cry aloud to You.

Daily Word

June 26

Owl Sparrow

"I am like an owl of the desert. I watch, and am as a sparrow alone upon the house top."

Psalm 102:6, 7

The owl is a bird of the night. It lives chiefly on the life of other creatures. It is not lovable, nor gentle in its habits. When you read in the Bible about the owl, think of thoughts that are false and destructive: and of the desert part of your heart from which they arise.

The sparrow is a small common bird. A picture of our more ordinary thoughts: sometimes merely natural, sometimes spiritual. A sparrow alone on the housetop is like a lonely thought, a spiritual one, for it is on the top of your house-the house of your mind.

Prayer

Hear my voice, O God, in my prayer:
preserve my life from fear of the enemy.

Daily Word

June 27

Scorpions

"Beware that you forget not the Lord your God who led you through that great and terrible wilderness wherein were fiery serpents and scorpions."

Deuteronomy 8:11, 15

This is a serious warning! We forget many things, but we should never forget the Lord. He alone leads us safely through the wilderness and its terrors.

The fiery serpents and the scorpions are the evil-destroying thoughts and feelings that creep cunningly about in our lower nature. False and evil persuasions often cause stupor to our minds just as the vile sting of a scorpion does to the body. The wilderness pictures our uncultivated mind, lacking in truth and in good.

Prayer

O Lord, You have delivered my soul from death, my eyes from tears, and my feet from falling.

Daily Word

June 28

Moses

"And there arose not a prophet since in Israel like Moses, whom the Lord knew face to face."

Deuteronomy 34:10

Moses was a great prophet. He was also a great leader; and his life was unusual both for its variety of experience and for the fact that he came to stand in a peculiarly close relationship to the Lord. We may recall that he was at first unwilling to accept the heavy responsibility which the Lord desired him to accept. We remember that Moses said, in Exodus 4:10, "O my Lord, I am not eloquent ... but I am slow of speech, and of a slow tongue."

That is often our reaction when the Lord calls us to perform a task which imposes a special responsibility upon us. We make excuses. Yet we have the Lord's reply, "Who has made man's mouth?" So it was that when Moses trusted the Lord and carried out his tasks the Lord upheld him so that even Pharoah stood in awe of this dread servant of the Lord. So may it be with us, if

Daily Word

we trust the Lord to uphold us when we serve Him. For His strength is more than enough for us, as it was for Moses.

Prayer

> *O Lord, open You my eyes, that I may behold wondrous things out of Your law.*

June 29

Elijah

"Behold, I will send you Elijah the prophet before the coming of the great and dreadful day of the Lord."

Malachi 4:5

Elijah was another great prophet of the Lord. His story in the Word is of outstanding interest. He is a splendid representative of the Lord, particularly of the Lord's Word.

It is the Lord's Word in its plain literal record that thus comes to prepare the way for Jesus. It comes to tell us of Him, and to introduce Him to us. It calls us to repentance of life, that we may receive Him. When we do, He stands before us in His Divine Human in every page of His opened Word: in lovely but terrible majesty.

Prayer

O Lord, deal with me according to Your mercy, and teach me Your statutes. I am Your servant, give me understanding, that I may know Your testimonies.

June 30

John Baptising

"I indeed baptise you with water unto repentance: but he that comes after me is mightier than I, whose shoes I am not worthy to bear: he shall baptise you with the Holy Spirit, and with fire."

Matthew 3:11

Our first baptism is by truth that leads to good: represented here by the waters of Jordan. John the Baptist represents the Word in its literal story, and the Jordan represents its truth, through which we must pass to enter the promised land. But Jesus, coming after is mightier: He comes to baptise us with the Holy Spirit and fire: it is baptism from within working outwards. The spirit is divine truth, and fire divine love. First we must be reformed, then regenerated.

Prayer

O Lord, teach me to do Your will; lead me into the land of uprightness.

Daily Word

July 1

Jesus and Temptation

"Then was Jesus led up of the Spirit into the wilderness to be tempted of the devil."

Matthew 4:1

In this account of Jesus, we have a picture of what happens to us, when we receive His spirit and love. Temptation does not come from the good spirit of God, but it does come as a result of receiving it. Directly we receive it there is conflict! The conscious presence of the Lord's good in our hearts immediately reveals the evils of our self-love. It is in this sense, that the spirit leads us into the wilderness: and while the two opposing positions are present there is bound to be temptation.

Prayer

O Lord, attend to my cry; for I am brought very low: deliver me from my persecutors: for they are stronger than I.

July 2

Jesus and Temptation

"And when he had fasted forty days and forty nights, he was afterwards hungered. And when the tempter came to Jesus and tempted him he said, If you be the Son of God, command that these stones be made bread."

Matthew 4:2, 3

Forty, in the Word, signifies temptation. Day and night represent its alternations. The children of Israel were forty years in the wilderness suffering intermittent temptations.

The tempter represents the hell of self-love, seeking to cast God out of our lives. Hunger may be natural, but it may also be deeply spiritual: when we suffer its affliction, Self says, Turn the stones of the wilderness into bread. These stones represent worldly deceits, but they can never satisfy us.

Prayer

Out of the depths have I cried to You, O Lord; let Your ears be attentive to the voice of my supplications.

Daily Word

July 3

Jesus and Temptation

"Jesus answered the tempter and said, It is written, Man shall not live by bread alone, but by every word that proceeds out of the mouth of God."

Matthew 4:4

Your body lives on food; the bread of this world. And you, who live in the body, need food too, but not of this world. You need spiritual food, for you are a spirit. You need this world's bread for your body, but you, the soul, need every word of the Lord, if you would live a healthy spiritual life in your body, and later in heaven. Jesus told the tempter this. Jesus is the Bread of Life. His words are spirit and life. Natural bread should not be used alone but together with spiritual bread.

Prayer

O Lord, you are my defence; and the rock of my refuge.

July 4

Jesus and Temptation

"Then the devil took Jesus up into the holy city, and set him on a pinnacle of the temple. And said to Him, If you are the Son of God, cast yourself down: for it is written, He shall give his angels charge concerning you: and in their hands they shall bear you up, lest at any time you dash your foot against a stone."

Matthew 4:5, 6

The tempter is now called "the devil". The temptation is deeper. The pinnacle of the temple represents pride of intelligence. This is what the devil inspires; and when he tells us to throw ourselves down and let the angels care for us, it means that our selfish love prompts us not to bother about practice, but to content ourselves by an empty profession of faith.

Prayer

Hear my prayer, O Lord, and let my cry come unto You.

Daily Word

July 5

Jesus and Temptation

"Again, the devil took him up into an exceeding high mountain, and showed him all the kingdoms of the world, and the glory of them; and says to him, All these things will I give you, if you fall down and worship me."

Matthew 4:8, 9

The exceeding high mountain is a picture of that which fills our hearts. Before we are regenerated, it is the love of self. From the love we have of ourselves we see all the things of the world below us, and want them. But when just a little truth from the Lord is present we know we must not fall down before these things, but lift them up and use them for Him.

Prayer

O Lord, keep my soul, and deliver me: let me not be ashamed; for I put my trust in You.

Daily Word

July 6

Jesus and Temptation

"Then Jesus said to him, Away with you, Satan: for it is written, You shall worship the Lord your God, and Him only shall you serve. Then the devil left him."

Matthew 4:10, 11

This is a splendid example for us.
Temptation comes, and we just turn to the Lord s Word. We find we must worship God and Him only. We tell Satan this, and send him hence, and he goes! Jesus came into the world to save sinners. He comes into your life to save you. He does it by loving you, and winning your love for Him.
Remember this, and tell the tempter you worship the Lord only; and he will leave you. Try it and you will know from experience.

Prayer

O Lord, it is good for me that I have been afflicted; that I might learn Your statutes.

Daily Word

July 7

Repentance

"From that time Jesus began to preach, and to say, Repent: for the kingdom of heaven is at hand."

Matthew 4:17

Repent! This is recorded as the first word, in the preaching of Jesus. But immediately, the reason is given. And what a momentous reason it is. Nothing less, than that the kingdom of heaven is at hand. At the door of your house, your mind. Ready to enter, and make your day. To give you divine teaching and divine love. To replace all that is drab, with vision and delight.

Repentance means earnestly turning from self to the Lord. As we do this we open the door, and heaven enters.

Prayer

O Lord, let my soul live. I have gone astray like a lost sheep; seek Your servant; for I do not forget Your commandments.

Daily Word

July 8

Jesus

"And Jesus went about all Galilee, teaching in their synagogues, and preaching the gospel of the kingdom, and healing all manner of sickness and all manner of disease among the people."

Matthew 4:23

Galilee is distant from Jerusalem. It represents our natural life which is distant from our spiritual life. After preaching repentance, Jesus goes about in every part of our own Galilee; to teach us, and preach the good news of heaven. Where He finds sickness and disease among our ideas, our thoughts and affections, He restores and heals. All that He did long ago, in Canaan, He does even now in us. In your life and mine.

Prayer

O Lord, because You have been my help, therefore in the shadow of Your wings will I rejoice. My soul follows hard after You.

July 9

Jesus

"And seeing the multitudes, Jesus went up into a mountain: and when he was settled, his disciples came to him: and he opened his mouth, and taught them."

Matthew 5:1, 2

Think of the multitudes as your ideas. Crowds and crowds of them; some concerned with your thinking and some with your feelings. Jesus sees and knows all about them.

Now think of the mountain, for just as mountains are the big things of natural life, so are the things you love most, the big things of your spirit-life. These form your heart, and this is where Jesus sits to teach you His love. The disciples who come to Him there, are those thoughts of yours that have answered His call and become disciples.

Prayer

Bow down Your ear, O Lord, hear me: for I am poor and needy.

July 10

Poor in Spirit

"Blessed are the poor in spirit: for theirs is the kingdom of heaven."

Matthew 5:3

This is the first blessing Jesus teaches on the mountain. It is also first in importance, the beginning of all the blessings. To be poor, is to be in need. To be poor in spirit, is to be in spiritual need. Need of any kind disposes us to accept help. The man who is proud and rich in himself, feels no need. He has no ability to receive the kingdom of heaven. He is full up, with himself.

The poor in spirit are humble, and know that of themselves they are empty of any good or any worth. Their need is like an open door, and heaven enters in.

Prayer

O Lord, open You my lips: and my mouth shall show forth Your praise.

July 11

Mourners

"Blessed are they that mourn: for they shall be comforted."

Matthew 5:4

We mourn when we lose someone or something we love. There is a feeling of pain and emptiness within us, and we are softened by the affliction. This is so whether we mourn naturally or spiritually.

When our hearts are softened, we are ready and able to receive comfort. Especially is this the case when the reason of our mourning in spiritual. We seem to have lost the love we had for the Lord. We have lost happiness.

We are in a strange land where we cannot sing the Lord's song. Realising this we mourn and are sad. Thus, the door is opened. The Lord enters and we are comforted.

Prayer

Lord, I cry to You: make haste to me; give ear to my voice, when I cry to You.

Daily Word

July 12

The Meek

"Blessed are the meek: for they shall inherit the earth."

Matthew 5:5

The Lord is creator: the earth is His. We, as His children, inherit the earth with all its wonder and loveliness. But to be properly His children we must be meek, that is, happily submissive to His will. There is a great difference between real inheritance, and mere so-called ownership by title deed. Spiritually understood, the earth represents our outer life, in which we live our Christian life. To be meek, is to be willing to learn of Jesus Who is meek and lowly in heart: then we inherit our earth instead of it inheriting us. This is very different from claiming our rights and entitlements.

Prayer

O Lord, grant that we may be meek and inherit the earth: and so delight ourselves in the abundance of peace.

Daily Word

July 13

Hunger

"Blessed are they which do hunger and thirst after righteousness: for they shall be filled."

> Matthew 5:6

We are happy indeed, when we suffer hunger and thirst for righteousness. For the need leads us to the supply. The food for the spiritually hungry is Jesus, The Bread of Life: and the drink of these who are spiritually thirsty is Jesus too, for He says, "If any man thirst, let him come unto Me and drink." The supply is unlimited and requires neither money nor price. But our capacity to receive is always related to our need. Thus we are happy and filled according to our hunger and thirst. It is through our hunger and thirst that the Lord leads us into the paths of righteousness.

Prayer

O Lord, satisfy the longing soul, and fill the hungry soul with goodness.

Daily Word

July 14

Mercy

"Blessed are the merciful: for they shall obtain mercy."

Matthew 5:7

Mercy! What hope and comfort it has brought to men and women. One of the loveliest qualities we can obtain. Mercy comes from good-will, hunting for good, never for evil. It is always seeking ways to temper pain and ease sorrow, to seek and to save the lost.

Mercy is one of the lovely qualities of the Lord's love. They are blessed who have it, and all can have it for the supply is abundant. The only limiting factor is the capacity to receive. Jesus tells us, Mercy obtains mercy: it crosses our threshold as we try to apply its qualities to others.

Prayer

O Lord, satisfy us in the morning with Your mercy: that we may rejoice and be glad all our days.

Daily Word

July 15

Pure in Heart

"Blessed are the pure in heart: for they shall see God."

Matthew 5:8

The pure in heart! These are they who ascend into the hill of the Lord.
Good health requires a pure physical heart: and ofcourse good spiritual health depends on a pure spiritual heart: a heart of pure love for God and the neighbour. This is the only kind of heart that opens our eyes to see God. And to see God is to be blessed in His hills of love. It is to see heaven and the beautiful qualities of God's love and wisdom. It is not just scholarship that opens the eyes, it is a pure heart.

Prayer

I will praise You, O Lord my God, with all my heart: and I will glorify Your name for evermore. For great is Your mercy toward me.

July 16

Peacemakers

"Blessed are the peacemakers: for they shall be called the children of God."

Matthew 5:9

Peacemakers! The children of God. People often very different from mere pacifists. Busy men and women, making peace, with the qualities of sincere love, patience and understanding. Seeking in all circumstances to bring good into life, by true thinking and usefulness.

Though we may not be able to do much in the world about us, we can be peacemakers in the little world of our own lives. We can compel ourselves to love God first and our neighbour as ourselves: in doing so we shall be actual makers of peace. And peacemakers, remember, are the children of God. Are you a peacemaker?

Prayer

O Lord, help us to depart from evil, and do good, to seek peace, and pursue it.

Daily Word

July 17

Persecution

"Blessed are they which are persecuted for righteousness' sake: for theirs is the kingdom of heaven."

Matthew 5:10

Righteousness is doing justly, loving mercy, and walking humbly with God. But directly we begin to exercise these qualities, the love we have for ourselves, and for worldly pleasures, molests us; and very soon we are persecuted for righteousness' sake. If we persist along the path of justice, mercy and humility, we shall suffer the tribulations of persecution, but we shall find the kingdom of heaven. Do you suffer persecution for the sake of righteousness? If you do, Jesus says, you are happy, for the kingdom of heaven belongs to you.

Prayer

O Lord my God, in You do I put my trust: save me from all them that persecute me, and deliver me.

July 18

Your Light

"Let your light so shine before men, that they may see your good works, and glorify your Father which is in heaven."

Matthew 5:16

What a blessing a light can be! But Jesus is speaking about your light. What is your light? It is the light that comes from what you love. You are a disciple of Jesus, so you love Him, and your light is from Him. It is this light you must shine, so that others can see the good it reveals: then they, like you, will glorify your Father in heaven.

An evil man shines his light on himself: a good man shines his light from his Father in heaven on to his neighbour.

Prayer

O Lord, let all those that seek You rejoice and be glad in You: let such as love Your salvation say continually, The Lord be magnified.

Daily Word

July 19

Yea, yea

"Let your Yes be Yes and you No, No: for whatever is more than these comes of evil."

Matthew 5:37

It is written: the people were astonished at the doctrine of Jesus. To many people this part of His doctrine is astonishing; for there are occasions when a simple positive yea, or nay, cannot be given: or so it seems.

Yet as we progress in our spiritual life we come much nearer to this position. We begin to know in our hearts that the answer must be, Yea, or Nay, as the case may be. We also begin to know that whatever is more, does indeed arise from evil - the evil of our own desires. Think it over.

Prayer

O Lord, through You will we push down our enemies: through Your name will we tread them under that rise up against us.

July 20

Enemies

"But I say to you, Love your enemies, bless those who curse you, do good to those that hate you, and pray for those which spitefully use you, and persecute you."

Matthew 5:44

Enemies are those who are against us. We are not told to agree with them, but we are told to love them. Even if our enemies curse, hate and persecute us, we are still to love, bless and pray for them. It is the teaching of Jesus, the doctrine of heaven. If you lived like this, you would be a happy as the angels. You would be one of the children of your Father who is in heaven. Nothing would disturb your inner peace.

Prayer

Lord, open tome the gates of righteousness: I will go into them, and I will praise the Lord.

Daily Word

July 21

Sincerity

"Take heed that ye do not your alms before men, to be seen of them: otherwise ye have no reward of your Father who is in heaven."

Matthew 6:1

Sincerity in religious life is of first importance. Our Father in heaven sees the heart. Others may see our acts of service; our alms or righteousness; but we are not to do them for this reason. The reward of our Father is, His acceptance of our love. It is also His truly wonderful love for us. When our righteousness is pretence, or only for the world to see, our Father's blessing is lost. We are to take heed about this; it is important!

Prayer

Help us, O God of our salvation, for the glory of Your name: and deliver us, and purge away our sins, for Your name's sake.

July 22

Praying

"When you pray, enter into your closet, and when you have shut your door, pray to your Father who is in secret; and your Father who sees in secret shall reward you openly."

Matthew 6:6

This is the Lord's teaching about prayer. The closet, or inner chamber, represents the interior of the mind. And shutting the door, means closing out all distracting thoughts from the world. In this secret place we meet, and talk with, our Father. Here He will see us, and reward us openly. When prayer begins from, and ends in, the outer life, it ceases there. When it begins from the inner chamber it spreads abroad, then the reward or love of our Father is open to all.

Prayer

Hear my prayer, O Lord, and give ear unto my cry, hold not Your peace at my tears.

July 23

Your Father

"Your Father knows what things you have need of, before you ask Him."

Matthew 6:8

At first this seems strange. If our Father knows our need, why ask? But when we think it over we see how good it is. How different it would be if He did not know! The truth is, our Father knows everything. Perhaps this is why He tells us we are not heard for much speaking.

To know when we pray that our Father understands our need is a great help. He is all powerful and eager to aid us, and only needs us to let Him in so that He can enclose us in His loving care. Then He sups with us, and communion is complete.

Prayer

Have mercy upon me, O God, according to Your loving kindness: according unto the multitudes of Your tender mercies.

Daily Word

July 24

Praying

"After this manner therefore pray ye."

Matthew 6:9

We all need to pray. But prayer is sometimes very difficult. It is easy to pray from a book: and it may sometimes be easy to say a lot of things to God. It is less easy to kneel down and talk to God as our Father intelligently. To feel His presence, and to know that He is listening. But it can be done by following the Lord's teaching. He does not tell us to pray in this way only, but He does clearly tell us to pray after this manner. The manner is brief, the words are simple, and the meaning is clear. And the prayer covers all our need.

Prayer

Teach me Your way, O Lord; then will I walk in Your truth: unite my heart to fear Your name.

Daily Word

July 25

Our Father

"Our Father who art in heaven."

Matthew 6:9

This is the beginning of the great prayer. We are talking to our Father. Not my Father, in an isolated sense, but our Father. The Father of us all, of every colour and every creed. We cannot begin this prayer selfishly: but only by taking with us all our brothers and sisters. As we do so we begin to feel round about us the Everlasting Arms.
Then immediately our thoughts are lifted to heaven, where He dwells. Perhaps for a moment we question, where is heaven? He tells us! The kingdom of heaven is within you. So we pray, closing our eyes to outside things and looking within, to the secret place of the Most High.

Prayer

O Lord, continue Your loving kindness unto them that know You.

Daily Word

July 26

Your Name

"Hallowed be your name."

Matthew 6:9

As we approach our Father in heaven we begin to feel His presence. Then we recognise a holy sphere and pray, "'hallowed be Your name". Perhaps for a moment we wonder, what is our Father's name? He has very many different names in the Bible. But one name stands out from all the others. It is the name the Bible says He shall be known by: You shall call His name Jesus, for He shall save His people from their sins. Jesus, the first and the last. The loveliest name human lips can frame. The name of our Father in His Divine Human form: hallowed by all His children.

Prayer

O Lord, all Your paths are mercy and truth. For Your name's sake, O Lord, pardon my iniquity; for it is great.

Daily Word

July 27

Your Kingdom

"Your Kingdom come."

Matthew 6:10

No kingdom can stand on anything less than compliance with its laws. Neither can the kingdom of heaven. To pray for it to come, is to pray for the sovereignty of our Father's teachings among men. These teachings are summed up in the two great commandments of love: love to our Father, and love to our neighbour. Where these are respected the Lord's kingdom comes. Where they are actually applied to life His kingdom is established.

It would be well sometimes to look in the mirror when you pray this prayer, for the person you see there, is the only one you can compel to receive the Lord's kingdom.

Prayer

You have dealt well with Your servant, O Lord, according to Your word. Teach me good judgement and knowledge: for I have believed Your commandments.

Daily Word

July 28

Your Will

"Your will be done in earth, as it is in heaven."

Matthew 6:10

The Lord's will is the will of divine love. It is the will to give His children joy and peace. To save all who are lost and broken: and to prepare homes for them in heaven. There is nothing we can pray for better than this. It is central in the prayer our Father has given us.

We are told to pray, that His will may be done in earth as it is in heaven. In heaven His will is supreme; when it is also supreme here, earth will be closely united with heaven: disease and sickness will vanish, and people will be happy.

Prayer

Unto You I lift up my eyes, O You that dwells in the heavens. O Lord have mercy upon us.

July 29

Daily Bread

"Give us this day our daily bread."

Matthew 6:11

Our daily bread! Without it, and what it represents, we cannot live. To maintain health the body must be regularly fed. But while we pray for this food, let us remember that we also need food for our religious life. The spirit needs regular feeding even as the body does. It must be well fed, and in good health, to press forward in the life of regeneration.

This bread our Father is telling us to pray for, is food for our souls. It is Jesus: for He says, "I am the Bread of Life." We need Him each day. How else can we love Him and our neighbour? He is our staff of life.

Prayer

O Lord, satisfy us early with Your mercy; that we may rejoice and be glad all our days.

Daily Word

July 30

Debts

"And forgive us our debts, as we forgive our debtors."

Matthew 6:12

To forgive, is to forget or remit. Here we ask our Father to forgive us, but only as we in turn forgive one another. But what are debts? Something we owe. What do we owe our Father? We owe Him the love of heart, soul, mind and strength, as His first commandment teaches.

In so far as this love is lacking we are in debt. And we owe love to our neighbour, equal to the love we have for ourselves: where this is wanting, we are in debt to one another. As we forgive our neighbour's debt, we can ask our Father to forgive us our debts.

Prayer

You, Lord, art good, and ready to forgive; and plentiful in mercy unto all them that call upon You.

Daily Word

July 31

Temptation

"And lead us not into temptation, but deliver us from evil."

Matthew 6:13

We do not like temptation, neither do we want to be in bondage to evil. So we pray as the Lord teaches. Yet, although the Lord does not lead us into temptation, He allows us to suffer its torments. It is the only way to freedom from the bondage of selfish desires. But if we pray to our Father for deliverance He will save us from being overcome. He will give us fortitude, patience and endurance: and at last evil will be cast out and we will be free. This new freedom will be like complete delivery from a horrible disease.

Prayer

From the end of the earth, O Lord, will I cry unto You, when my heart is overwhelmed: lead me to the rock that is higher than I.

Daily Word

August 1

Treasures

"Do not lay up for yourselves treasures upon earth, where moth and rust corrupt, and thieves break in and steal."

Matthew 6:19

Treasures are things you love. The earth represents your outer life. Moth and rust represent evil things and false things, respectively; things that corrupt and spoil.
Thieves are evil desires that break into your treasures and rob you of their delight. In this way treasures laid on the earth soon lose all their appeal. You may accumulate them, bother about them, and find a place to store them, but in the end they cannot give you any happiness. They are of the earth, earthy, and soon return to dust.

Prayer

Lord, make me to know my end, and the measure of my days, what it is: that I may know how frail I am.

Daily Word

August 2

Treasures

"But lay up for yourselves treasures in heaven, where neither moth nor rust corrupts, and where thieves do not break through nor steal. For where your treasure is, there will your heart be also."

Matthew 6:20, 21

Many people seem to live to collect things. All sorts of things: antiques, stamps, and even cigarette cards. But all for this world alone.

Jesus tells us to collect things too; He calls them treasures. Treasures that can never be corrupted, never be stolen. Treasures we can lay up in heaven and take with us when we leave this world. They are the treasures of love and kindness, and knowledge of the Lord; sweet and happy memories, unforgettable experiences.

Prayer

O Lord, continue Your loving kindness unto them that know You; and Your righteousness unto the upright in heart.

Daily Word

August 3

Raiment

"Why take ye thought for raiment? Consider the lilies of the field, how they grow; they toil not, neither do they spin. And yet I say to you, that even Solomon in all his glory was not arrayed like one of these."

Matthew 6:28, 29

Raiment is important. But spiritual raiment is of greater importance. The lilies of the field, so sweetly beautiful are a picture of innocence. As we consider their growth we recognise their correspondence. They grow so patiently and quietly, and are quite innocent of their loveliness.

They do not toil to spin their raiment. Their quality is the gift of divine Love. Even wisdom in all its glory is not arrayed like innocence. Innocence is celestial.

Prayer

Lord, keep back Your servant from presumptuous sins: then shall I be innocent from the great transgression.

Daily Word

August 4

Seeking

"Seek ye first the kingdom of God, and His righteousness; and all these things shall be added unto you."

Matthew 6:33

It is one thing to be first in time, and another to be first in importance. The kingdom of God is of first importance. It should be the first purpose in all that we do. We should seek it in all our propositions and activities; for it is the kingdom of divine Wisdom and divine Love. When we give it first place and make it our end in life, then all the other things we need fall into place and are added unto us. Anything less than the Lord's Kingdom in the first place is of inferior value, and a continuing loss to us.

Prayer

O Lord, You have prepared Your throne in the heavens: and Your kingdom rules over all.

Daily Word

August 5

Judging

"Judge not, that ye be not judged. For with what judgement ye judge, ye shall be judged."

Matthew 7:1, 2

How easy it is to judge! But how difficult to judge wisely and kindly. And as we judge others we set up a standard that in turn judges us.

Judgement as to whether an act or quality is good or bad, is often necessary. But judgement of a person, or a person's motive, is forbidden. Among God's children, it is strictly avoided. Our Father alone can truly judge, for He sees the hearts of men and knows all their intentions. His judgement too is filled with loving kindness and tender mercies.

Prayer

Have mercy upon me, O God, according to Your loving kindness: according unto the multitude of Your tender mercies blot out my transgressions.

Daily Word

August 6

Asking

"Ask, and it shall be given you; seek, and you shall find; knock, and it shall be opened to you."

Matthew 7:7

Life largely consists, from early childhood, of these three things. We seem to be always asking questions: and seeking for this and that; and all our learning is a kind of knocking. We know that unless we ask, and make an effort, we shall be left behind in all our undertakings.

But do we realise that these things are even more important in spiritual life? Jesus will give us the Bread of Life, if we ask Him. If we seek we shall find Him, and if we knock at the door of His Word He will open it up to us.

Prayer

Show me Your ways, O Lord; teach me Your paths.

August 7

Conduct

"All things whatsoever ye would that men should do to you, do ye even so to them: for this is the law and the prophets."

Matthew 7:12

How direct and clear the Lord's teaching is. What could be better than this? Simply treat others as you would like them to treat you. It is the conduct of heaven brought to the earth. It is the law and the prophets, because it is the truth, leading to the goodness of life.

Within your soul where heaven is, you know it is true and good. You know that if you let this teaching down into your earth life, and make it your law of neighbourly love, then you will be living as the angels do.

Prayer

O Lord, You have beset me behind and before, and laid Your hand upon me.

August 8

The Gate

"Enter ye in at the strait gate: for wide is the gate, and broad is the way, that leads to destruction, and many there be which go in by it."

Matthew 7:13

In general before each of us there are two gates. This is where our freedom lies. We can choose this or that without any outside compulsion. One is narrow and difficult, but it leads to life. The other is called wide because it admits no restraints: it leads to a broad way where many enter, and journey together to destruction.

Which is your choice? Tell yourself the answer! Truth is the strait or narrow gate; false desires the wide one.

Prayer

Open to me the gates of righteousness: I will go into them, and I will praise You, Lord. Save me, I ask You, O Lord.

August 9

Fruits

"Wherefore by their fruits ye shall know them."

Matthew 7:20

This is true everywhere, but here Jesus is talking of men. Men are not known by their affectation, but by the way they live. Their daily activities are their fruits. But not only do we know others by their fruits; we can also know ourselves by the same test. We can even look in the mirror, and see something of our fruits in the face that looks back at us. For the face is an index to the man behind it.

Our actions are fruits, so are our habits. We can, from time to time, examine these, and so know the quality of the life we live, from the fruits we yield.

Prayer

O Lord, make Your face to shine upon Your servant: save me for Your mercies' sake.

August 10

Lord, Lord!

"Not everyone that says to me, Lord, Lord, shall enter into the kingdom of heaven; but he that does the will of my Father which is in heaven."

Matthew 7:21

Heaven is the home of those who truly love the Lord. It is not gained by favour, or by crying, Lord, Lord! To live there one must be happy to do the will of the Father in heaven: and to serve and love others, at least equally, as oneself. Heaven is not composed of people who have managed to gain admittance; but of men and women who love to live as the Lord teaches. Of people to whom the joy of life is to serve others.

Prayer

Let all those that seek You, Lord, rejoice and be glad in You: let such as love Your salvation say continually, The Lord be magnified.

Daily Word

August 11

A Wise Man

"Therefore whoever hears these sayings of mine, and does them, I will liken him to a wise man, who built his house upon a rock."

Matthew 7:24

If you hear, and do as Jesus says, He will liken you to a wise man. A wise man who built his house on a rock. The sayings of Jesus are the Wisdom of divine Love.

The house built on a rock represents the character established on the foundations of eternal truth-the Wisdom of God. Our first concern should be to listen to the Lord; and our next, to put what we hear into practice. Then even you and I will be likened to a wise man.

Prayer

From the end of the earth will I cry to You, when my heart is overwhelmed: lead me to the rock that is higher than I.

Daily Word

August 12

Floods

"And the rain descended, and the floods came, and the winds blew, and beat upon that house; and it fell not: for it was founded upon a rock."

Matthew 7:25

Rain corresponds to God's truth falling as a blessing from heaven. But in an opposite sense, as in this teaching, it represents an outpouring of false ideas.

These, gathering together, form floods of evil. The wind beating them against the house is the spirit of evil, trying to wreck man's mind. But the rock of truth on which the house of the mind is built cannot be overthrown. Build on the sayings of Jesus, and your house will be invincible!

Prayer

O Lord, open You my eyes that I may behold wondrous things out of Your law. I am a stranger in the earth: hide not Your commandments from me.

Daily Word

August 13

Doctrine

"And it came to pass, when Jesus had ended these sayings, the people were astonished at his doctrine."

Matthew 7:28

The doctrine of Jesus and the astonishment of the people. The sayings of Jesus contain the teaching of Jesus, here spoken of as His "doctrine". This doctrine came to the people with new authority. It was clearly defined and very direct. The people had heard nothing like it before; it simply astonished them.

It would astonish the world today, if folk would listen to it, and fallow its directions. It would astonish you if you took it to heart: when lived it changes men and women. It is the code that distinguishes Christians by revealing the difference between religion and religiosity.

Prayer

Teach me Your way, O Lord; I will walk in Your truth: and unite my heart to fear Your name.

Daily Word

August 14

Jesus

"When Jesus was come down from the mountain, great multitudes followed him."

Matthew 8:1

Comparatively few people ascend high into the mountains. Those who do, know their majesty and loveliness. Spiritual mountains are lovelier still: they are elevations of love beyond the worldly level. Only a few of our thoughts are able to ascend to these altitudes. These thoughts of ours that do, are the Lord's disciples in our minds. Through these the Lord teaches us how to live the life that leads to heaven.

When Jesus comes down in His teaching to meet us, and be with us in the ordinary things of life then multitudes of our feelings and thoughts follow Him.

Prayer

Let the people praise You, O God; then shall the earth yield her increase; and God, even our own God, shall bless us.

Daily Word

August 15

Evening

"When the evening was come, they brought to Jesus many that were possessed with devils: and he cast out the devils with his word, and healed all that were sick."

Matthew 8:16

This makes such happy reading. Devils cast out, and all the sick healed. What an evening to remember. But it has a direct message for you and me as well.

The evening represents a declining state of spiritual experience. The devils are evil passions that enter into us, and the sick represent the evil consequences. Jesus casting out devils with His word reveals the wonderful power of His teaching; which when applied to life removes our evil passions. And when these are removed our spiritual sickness is healed.

Prayer

Be pleased, O Lord, to deliver me: O Lord, make haste to help me.

August 16

Follow Me

"And another of his disciples said to him, Lord, suffer me first to go and bury my father. But Jesus said to him, Follow me; and let the dead bury their dead."

Matthew 8:21, 22

How strange this sounds. Think of the "disciple" as one who follows the Lord; or as a principle in your life that does so. Then think of the father, not as a person but as the old Adam within, the parent not of our new birth but of all our selfish nature. This dies when we fallow Jesus, and we need not linger over our loss. Jesus says, Let the dead bury their dead. By the dead is represented self-love, the father of all our troubles. Self-love is a dead thing and always buries itself.

Prayer

O Lord of hosts, blessed is the man that trusts in You.

August 17

The Ship

"And when he was entered into a ship, his disciples followed him."

        Matthew 8:23

Can you see the ship with Jesus and the disciples, sailing on the Sea of Galilee? Can you see it again as the little ship of your faith? Your faith, into which Jesus has entered to journey with you from the world to heaven. Long ago we used to sing:

"We are out on the ocean sailing To a land beyond the tide."

This is just what all the disciples of Jesus are doing. And remember, that you as an individual, have disciples of Jesus in your own mind. All the feelings and thoughts that look to Him are your own disciples, that follow Him.

Prayer

O Lord, whom have I in heaven but You?
And there is none upon earth that I desire beside You.

Daily Word

August 18

The Tempest

"And behold, there arose a great tempest in the sea, insomuch that the ship was covered with the waves: but he was asleep."

Matthew 8:24

The sea has so many moods! Sometimes calm and delightful, at others wild and tempestuous: and between these extremes a wide range of varying conditions, with flowing currents and tides.

It is a picture of our natural life, through which we must pass to gain a home in heaven. Sometimes our natural life is very disturbed, and even tempestuous. Waves of difficulties and troubles hit our little ship of faith, and almost cover us with despair. We forget Jesus. He seems to be asleep and to have no share in our troubles.

Prayer

Had not You, Lord, been on our side, the waters had overwhelmed us, the stream had gone over our soul.

August 19

Save us

"And his disciples came to Jesus, and awoke him, saying, Lord, save us: we perish."

Matthew 8:25

We perish! It is a cry of despair. It is a picture of experience we all suffer at one time or another. We can hardly pass through the struggle of regeneration without doing so. Our self-will must be softened.

But blessed are the uses of adversity:

they drive us to Jesus. We go to Him and awake Him. Actually this is an appearance. The Lord neither slumbers nor sleeps in His care of us: it is we who were asleep. But the storm of trouble brings us to our senses. In our desperate need we cry out, "Save us: we perish."

Prayer

Turn us again, O God, and cause Your face to shine,· and we shall be saved.

August 20

A great calm

"And he says to them, why are you fearful, O you of little faith? Then He arose, and rebuked the winds and the sea; and there was a great calm."

Matthew 8:26

A great calm! What a welcome and wonderful experience after the tempest.

But the question: Why are ye fearful, O ye of little faith? What is our answer? Perhaps just that-our little faith! But quickly, our faith grows bigger, for Jesus arises within us, and rebukes the winds, and sea, of our troubled state. Our little ship of faith regains an even keel. There is a great calm, and with the calm comes a foretaste of the peace that Jesus gives, that passes all understanding.

Prayer

O Lord, still the noise of the seas, and the tumult of Your people.

Daily Word

August 21

They marvelled

"But the men marvelled, saying, What manner of man is this, that even the winds and the sea obey him."

Matthew 8:27

No wonder the men marvelled! Just a few words from Jesus, and the storm gives place to a great calm.

So is it with our storm-tossed lives. Faith in Jesus makes all the difference. We marvel again and again at the way He looks after us. We cannot understand His Providence: it is infinite. What manner of man is this? He is God, revealed in His divine humanity, having power over all the winds and seas of adversity that afflict us. He is Jesus, the first and the last.

Prayer

Show Your marvellous loving kindness, O You that saves by Your right hand them which put their trust in You from those that rise up against them.

Daily Word

August 22

Heavy laden

"Come unto me, all ye that labour and are heavy laden, and I will give you rest."

Matthew 11:28

Are you troubled with the toil of life? If you will respond to this appeal you will have rest.

But how can you come to Jesus? Well, it is as real a journey as any other. You cannot leave one position for a new one without covering the intervening distance.

What is the distance from you to Jesus? It is not physical: it cannot be measured by miles. It is surely a distance of desire. If you desire only your own way, then you are far from Him. But if you love Him, then you are coming to Him, and He will give you rest.

Prayer

Keep me, O Lord, according to Your loving kindness. Your word is true from the beginning.

August 23

Learn of Me

"Take my yoke upon you, and learn of me; for I am meek and lowly in heart: and ye shall find rest for your souls."

Matthew 11:29

This means, replacing the yoke of self-desire, with the yoke of the Lord's will. But to do this we must know what the Lord's will is: so Jesus says, Learn of me. As we do learn, we come to know His will is love. His wonderful love for us, and the love He wants us to give Him, and our neighbour. This love is meek and lowly, full of charity and service to others: free from aggression and self-importance.

In it, is innocence and rest for the soul.

Prayer

O Lord, so teach us to number our days, that we may apply our hearts unto wisdom.

August 24

My yoke

"For my yoke is easy, and my burden is light."

Matthew 11:30

Love makes all things easy. It can ease burdens and reduce strain, and soothe sorrows. The Lord's yoke is easy just because it is love. It is this yoke of love that Jesus asks us to take upon ourselves, that we might have rest. And His burden is the teaching, or truth, of His Word. It is light, because its heart is love and loving kindness: and because His truth makes us free and shows us how to walk in a plain path. And because, without any effort or toil of our own it defends us securely from evil and its horrors.

Prayer

Let Your mercies come also unto me, O Lord, even Your salvation, according to Your word. And I will delight myself in Your commandments.

Daily Word

August 25

Like Sheep

"Behold, I send you forth as sheep in the midst of wolves: be ye therefore wise as serpents, and harmless as doves."

Matthew 10:16

Like sheep in the midst of wolves! Sheep represent something good, and wolves something evil and rapacious. In this world they seem to be mixed together, but actually the sheep are as Jesus says, in the midst. And they are to be wise like serpents yet harmless as doves. Serpents represent sensual principles which are subtle, and doves good and holy principles quite free from harm. As this applies to the world at large, so it applies to the little world of your own life. The sheep must be in the midst, prudent as serpents but harmless as doves.

Prayer

O Lord, help us to know that we are Your people and the sheep of Your pasture.

Daily Word

August 26

Enduring

"He that endures to the end shall be saved."

Matthew 10:22

Endurance is a great quality. One of the greatest. The end is a completion of a task: the cause of all effort. But what are we to be saved from? Not from God for He is love, and love harms no one. Not from anyone, or anything, outside of us: these can only hurt the body which will die in any case. The only thing that can make hell for us, is the love of self, instead of the love of God. It can lead us into horrible states of misery and unhappiness.

To endure to the end, is to endure the temptations, and the trials of the journey from the love of self to the love of God.

Prayer

Create in me a clean heart, O God

August 27

Body and Soul

"Fear not them which kill the body, but are not able to kill the soul."

Matthew 10:28

Your soul is you! Your body is your covering in this natural world. You will live always, but your natural body, after having served its worldly purpose will die. As the body is temporary we need not worry too much about it.

But the soul is different: it cannot be killed. But it can miss its way. It can be degraded and lose its happiness; and so drawn by sin against God down into hell. We should certainly fear every desire and every thought that is against God. These can cast us into hell.

Prayer

Keep me, O Lord, from the hands of the wicked: preserve me from the violent man; who have purposed to overthrow my goings.

August 28

Hairs

"The very hairs of your head are all numbered."

Matthew 10:30

It seems incredible! Millions of people, and the hairs of the head of relatively little importance. But actually this is just the point of the saying. The Divine Providence has regard to the least and most ordinary of circumstances.

Out of all the millions of men and women, Providence knows you. Knows your sorrows and your joys, your most insignificant feelings and thoughts. All are numbered, all accounted for, in every step of your way. You cannot understand, it can you? But it makes no difference, it is God's teaching and it is true. You are finite: Your Lord is infinite.

Prayer

How precious are Your thoughts to me, O God! how great is the sum of them! If I should count them they are more in number than the sand.

Daily Word

August 29

Sword

"Think not that I am come to send peace on earth; I came not to send peace but a sword."

Matthew 10:34

Peace and the sword are two opposites. Yet how often it is said one prepares the way for the other.

But what is spoken of here is spiritual peace, and a spiritual sword. Spiritual peace cannot be on the earth, till the sword of the Lord's truth has prepared the way: till His truth has removed the falsities of self-domination, and driven away peace-destroying pursuits. How can peace dwell with feverish passions and self-importance? Truth must first provide a vessel in which peace can dwell.

Prayer

Hear my cry, O God; from the end of the earth will I cry to You, when my heart is overwhelmed: lead me to the rock that is higher than I.

Daily Word

August 30

Foes

"A man's foes shall be they of his own household."

Matthew 10:36

At first reading this seems wrong. The commandments tell us to honour our parents and to love one another; how then are we to find our foes in our own house? Well, spiritually understood foes are not people, but desires and thoughts. And our household does not refer to a merely natural dwelling, but to one's own mind.

Your mind is your household, containing many affections or desires, and a multitude of thoughts. Among these desires and thoughts, are some that are opposed to God, and His love and truth; these are the foes of your very own household. They are relentless and cruel, and friends of hell.

Prayer

I will extol You, O Lord; for You have lifted me up, and not made my foes to rejoice over me.

Daily Word

August 31

His Cross

"He that takes not his cross, and follows after me, is not worthy of me."

Matthew 10:38

To be worthy is to be worthwhile. Spiritually, we take our cross, by loving the Lord's Divine Truth, which denies us the love of self first." It is this surrender of self-will and all the merely worldly pleasures that arise from it, that make our cross. When we take it up and follow the Lord, we become more closely conjoined to Him. And it is only conjunction with Him, that can make us worthy of His name. Cross carrying is hard at first, but it leads to worthwhile life, and the greatest possible happiness.

Prayer

In You, O Lord, do I put my trust; let me never be ashamed: deliver me in Your righteousness. O lead me and guide me.

September 1

Corn

"At that time Jesus went on the sabbath day through the corn; and his disciples were all hungered, and began to pluck the ears of corn, and to eat."

> Matthew 12:1

It is a beautiful picture of the sabbath day. Jesus and the disciples amid the corn. Perhaps it recalls memories for you when in days past you, like the disciples, have walked along a path through the corn.

The sabbath represents a state of peace, and the corn the food the Lord gives us in His Word. The disciples are those who love the Lord; and their hunger signifies their need of Him. Plucking and eating the ears of corn is what we do when we feed on the Word of life.

Prayer

God be merciful to us, and bless us; and cause His face to shine upon us.

Daily Word

September 2

The Hand

"Then says he to the man, Stretch forth your hand. And he stretched it forth; and it was restored whole, like as the other."

Matthew 12:13

But for a little stretching we would miss many good things. How often we stretch out till we can just grasp what we want. We do so physically and mentally. And always it is desire that makes us bother to stretch.
It is much the same in our spiritual life, but if desire fails we cannot stretch. Then through lack of use our hand withers. But if in response to Jesus, we stretch out to Him, our hand is restored. We again have power to stretch and reach, because we desire to obey the Lord.

Prayer

O Lord, establish You the work of our hands upon us; yea, the work of our hands establish You it.

Daily Word

September 3

He spoke and saw

"Then was brought to Him one possessed with a devil, blind, and dumb: and He healed him, insomuch that the blind and dumb both spoke and saw."

Matthew 12:22

Think of it! One possessed with a devil, and blind and dumb. Supposing it was you! How wonderful it would be to meet Jesus and to be healed.

When our personal control is in the grip of hell we are possessed. And when we are blind spiritually our understanding cannot see, or reason: then we are also spiritually dumb for we cannot speak the Lord's truth. Jesus can heal us because He can drive the devil out, and when the devil goes Jesus enters. Then we can talk and see.

Prayer

O Lord, satisfy us early with Your mercy, that we may rejoice and be glad all our days.

Daily Word

September 4

Whoever has

"For whoever has, to him shall be given, and be shall have more abundance: but whoever has not, from him shall be taken away even that he has."

Matthew 13:12

This seems hard. Yet it is a lesson that life teaches us. Give a piece of land a bushel of seed, and the harvest will be an abundance more. Acquire a knowledge of letters and you will soon be able to read the wisdom of the ages. With labour and diligence everything you have increases. So does knowledge and love of the Lord, till your cup runs over.

Be indolent; plant no seed; and soon your little land loses what it had, and becomes a wilderness. Refuse to learn; and your mind becomes empty. Repel the Lord's love; and your happiness will be taken away.

Prayer

O Lord, my soul faints for Your salvation.

Daily Word

September 5

Merchant man

"Again, the kingdom of heaven is like a merchant man, seeking goodly pearls."

Matthew 13:45

A merchant man! What a variety of merchants there are. Coal merchants, timber merchants and many others. But how nice to be a pearl merchant.

The kingdom of heaven is like a pearl merchant. Always interested in goodly pearls: and seeking for them with continuous delight. The good pearls are the experiences of the Lord's love, and the delightful knowledges of His wisdom. These form the universal commerce of heaven.

If you like you can be a pearl merchant, and deal in the precious pearls of the Lord's Word. Then one day you may find the pearl of great price.

Prayer

Hear me, O Lord; for Your loving kindness is good: turn to me according to the multitude of Your tender mercies.

Daily Word

September 6

Pearls

"Who, when he had found one pearl of great price, went and sold all that he had, and bought it."

Matthew 13:46

This is the peak of discovery, and the merchant's greatest triumph.

The pearl of great price is the know ledge and acknowledgement of Jesus. In heaven, He is first and last, the Lamb in the midst of the throne. To find Him is the greatest task in life. But we cannot take Him home as ours, without paying the purchase price. What is it? No figure is stated, none can be. The price is heavy, very heavy; nevertheless it is within the reach of rich and poor alike. It is nothing less than all we have. Complete exchange of me, for Him.

Prayer

Be You my portion, O Lord: I entreat Your favour with my whole heart.

September 7

The Net

"Again, the kingdom of heaven is like a net, that was cast into the sea, and gathered of every kind."

Matthew 13:47

Have you ever thought of this, in relation to yourself? It affects others, but in particular it is about you. Heaven casts a net into the sea of your own little life. It does so to catch all that it can for your eternal home. It gathers of every kind: good affections and mean ones, true thoughts and false thoughts. All mixed together in the sea of your earthly life. Like the tares growing together in a field of corn, all must be harvested together, that the good may be saved.

Prayer

Consider and hear me, O Lord my God: lighten my eyes, lest I sleep the sleep of death: let me rejoice in Your salvation.

Daily Word

September 8

Full Nets

"Which, when it (the net) was full, they drew to shore, and sat down, and gathered the good into vessels, but cast the bad away."

Matthew 13:48

Just as fishermen draw their nets in, and sort out their catch, so the heaven within us draws in its nets. Draws them in for the same reason, to secure and save all the good and true fish it can. For there are spiritual fish; they are the affections and thoughts that live in the waters of our earth life. Some are of value to heaven, and the home that is being prepared for us there. But the bad or useless ones are cast away.

Prayer

O Lord, continue Your loving kindness unto them that know You, and Your righteousness to the upright in heart. Let not the hand of the wicked remove me.

September 9

End of the World

"So shall it be at the end of the world: the angels shall come forth, and sever the wicked from among the just, and shall cast them into the furnace of fire."

Matthew 13:49, 50

Again, think of this in relation to yourself. When your natural, world-life ends your heaven will take over. As wicked passions and thoughts would spoil it, they must be eliminated. This is a task for the angels who are God's messengers. They live in truth and are able to make proper discrimination. Every good or just affection is saved, also every true thought. These are the treasures you have laid up for heaven. Every wicked thing is cast out and burned.

Prayer

O Lord my God, in You do I put my trust: save me from all them that persecute me, and deliver me.

Daily Word

September 10

Compassion

"And Jesus went forth, and saw a great multitude, and was moved with compassion toward them, and he healed their sick."

Matthew 14:14

A great multitude! How often we read that Jesus had compassion. It is the feeling of divine love for the broken and sick. Inside the borders of your life there are great multitudes: not of peoples, but of the milling feelings and thoughts that people represent. Jesus sees them all as He comes forth in His love for you. He sees how sad and sick many of your appetites and ideas are, and He enters into you to heal them. Every least thing of your mind is watched over.

Prayer

Save us, O Lord our God, and gather us from among the heathen, to give thanks to Your holy name, and to triumph in Your praise.

September 11

A desert place

"And when it was evening his disciples came to him, saying, this is a desert place, and the time is now past; send the multitude away, that they may go into the villages, and buy themselves victuals."

Matthew 14:15

Just as evening signifies the decline of a day, so does it signify the decline of a spiritual state. After sunset night soon follows, and spiritually we find we are in a desert place. It is then that our disciples, or thoughts that follow Jesus, go to Him. and complain. For the multitudes of things there are in our natural life are tired and hungry: and we ask Jesus to send them away. We want them to satisfy their hunger in their villages: that is, in the outside things to which they are accustomed.

Prayer
Let my cry come before You, O Lord.

Daily Word

September 12

Five loaves

"But Jesus said to them, They need not depart; give them to eat. And they say to him, we have here but five loaves, and two fishes."

Matthew 14:16, 17

They need not depart! Give ye them to eat, says Jesus. But there are multitudes of people, and they have only five loaves and two fishes. There are multitudes of things in your mind, all of them hungry and many weary. But they have followed Jesus and He does not want them to return to their ordinary natural pursuits without food.

The five loaves represent the little affections for the Lord remaining to them as night begins to fall; and the two fishes represent their little faith.

Prayer

When I said, My foot slips: Your mercy, O Lord, held me up. In the multitude of my thoughts within me Your comforts delight my soul.

Daily Word

September 13

He blessed

"And he commanded the multitude to sit down on the grass, and took the five loaves, and the two fishes, and looking up to heaven, he blessed, and brake and gave the loaves to the disciples, and the disciples to the multitude."

Matthew 14:19

Jesus took the very little love and faith they had for Him. Then looking to heaven, He blessed and broke it into many parts. Thus a little good in the hands of Jesus becomes an abundance, for it is as a vessel which He fills to overflowing with His love. This divine food is passed to the thousands of things that compose our ordinary outer life by means of the disciples. The disciples are our spiritual principles that follow Jesus: they are the medium between our internal and external life.

Prayer

In the day of my trouble I will call upon You, O Lord: for You answer me.

Daily Word

September 14

They did all eat

"And they did all eat, and were filled: and they took up of the fragments that remained twelve baskets full. And they that had eaten were about five thousand men, beside women and children."

Matthew 14:20, 21

It is wonderful! All the things that compose our life are now filled. No part is unsatisfied. Give Jesus a little love and He will give you an abundance, even to preparing a table before you in the wilderness. The twelve baskets full of fragments, after all had eaten, represent the fullness of the knowledge of God's goodness and truth, resulting from our feeding on the bread that He gives us.

Prayer

O Lord, all wait upon You, that You may give them their meat in due season. You open Your hand, they are filled with good.

September 15

Whoever

"Then said Jesus to his disciples ... whoever will save his life shall lose it: and whoever will lose his life for my sake shall find it."

Matthew 16:24, 25

Man's life, spoken of here, refers to his natural life in the world, and to the life he has in his body. To make this an end, and to live for it, is to put self first. They who do this lose it, for its end is deadly both as to body and soul. But those who deny self, and follow Jesus, find true life and live for ever. They lose the life of worldly gratification, but in doing so they find true life, that is filled more and more with eternal delight.

Prayer

O Lord, continue Your loving kindness to them that know You; and Your righteousness to the upright in hearing.

Daily Word

September 16

Transfigured

"And (Jesus) was transfigured before them: and his face did shine as the sun, and his raiment was white as the light."

Matthew 17:2

To the disciples Jesus seemed different. But actually He was not changed. But Peter, James and John were seeing Jesus with their spirit-eyes, opened especially for the purpose. His face shining as the sun represents the glory of His divine love, and His raiment being as white as the light represents the truth of His love. Jesus is indeed the Sun of heaven.

"Sun of my soul, you saviour dear,
It is not night if You be near."

Prayer

God be merciful to us, and bless us; and cause His face to shine upon us; that Your way may be known upon earth, Your saving health among all nations.

Daily Word

September 17

Jesus only

"And when they had lifted up their eyes, they saw no man, save Jesus only."

Matthew 17:8

No wonder! They had just seen Jesus in the glory of His Divine Humanity. After this, when they lift up their eyes they will see Jesus only: Jesus the First and the Last. Jesus, King of Kings and Lord of Lords. He alone will be their vision, their Father and Saviour.

When once a man has seen Jesus everything is changed. The eyes of his understanding are filled with the vision: relatively speaking he sees no other but Him. He must look down into the things of the world, but when the eyes of his spirit are lifted up, it will be the face of Jesus, the Sun of heaven, he will behold.

Prayer

In You, O Lord, do I put my trust: You are my strong refuge.

Daily Word

September 18

Faith

"And Jesus said to them ... Truly I say to you, If you have faith as a grain of mustard seed, you shall say to this mountain, move; and it shall move; and nothing shall be impossible to you."

Matthew 17:20

Faith! What is it? Faith is the eye of love. It is given to those who acknowledge the Lord, learn of Him from the Word, and live according to His teaching. This faith secures the presence of the Lord, and saves us from ourselves. Even when it is only in its beginning, and small as a grain of mustard seed, it enables us to remove mountains of selfishness. Indeed, such faith, because it gives us God's presence, makes nothing impossible unto us.

Prayer

O God, You are my God; early will I seek You: my soul thirsts for You.

September 19

Greatest?

"At the same time came the disciples to Jesus, saying, Who is the greatest in the kingdom of heaven?"

Matthew 18:1

The question is astonishing. The answer Jesus gave them, must have seemed even more astonishing. Among the children of the Lord greatness stands for love. Not for eminence as mankind understands it. Not for power and might and distinction. Jesus told us to learn of Him because He was meek and lowly in heart. In heaven he is greatest who loves greatly-who can love others more than himself, and wants to be servant of all.

People in heaven don't think about being great or of importance. All there are brothers and sisters, children of the Heavenly Father.

Prayer

Our Father which art in heaven, Hallowed be Your name. Your kingdom come. Your will be done in earth, as it is in heaven.

Daily Word

September 20

A child

"And Jesus called a little child unto him,
and set him in the midst of them."

> Matthew 18:2

A little child represents a little innocence. This is what Jesus calls unto Him. Innocence is the beginning of good spiritual life. To be innocent is to be free from self-will: it is to acknowledge the Lord as Father, and to love to do His will.

In the depths of your mind you will find if you seek, the little child of long ago. And there in the memories of your infancy you will recall states of innocence: they are still there in the midst of your life. It is through these precious remains that the Lord will save you from yourself.

Prayer

*So teach us, Lord, to remember our days,
that we may apply our hearts unto wisdom.*

September 21

Converted

"Jesus said, Truly I say to you, unless you become as little children, you shall not enter into the kingdom of heaven."

Matthew 18:3

This is the teaching of Jesus about being converted. We are to turn and become as little children. If we do not, we will not be able to enter the kingdom of heaven.

In the Word little children represent innocence. To be converted and become like them, means that we must cease to be led by ourselves. Our activities must be innocent of self; otherwise we cannot enter the Lord's kingdom where He alone is Lord. Thus we daily pray, "Your will be done."

Prayer

Keep back Your servant, Lord, from presumptuous sins, let them not have dominion over me: then shall I be upright, and I shall be innocent from the great transgression.

Daily Word

September 22

Humble himself

"Whoever therefore shall humble himself as this little child, the same is the greatest in the kingdom of heaven. And whoso shall receive one such little child in my name receives me."

Matthew 18:4, 5

To humble ourselves as a little child is to love the Lord as our Father. This is innocence. It is the greatest quality in heaven. To receive one such little child, is to receive the Lord Himself: for where innocence is, the Lord is in the centre. Th us we read, The Lamb who is in the midst of the throne, shall feed them, and shall lead them unto living fountains of waters.

The Lamb represents divine innocence.

Prayer

Lord, You have heard the desire of the humble: You prepare their heart, You cause Your ear to hear.

September 23

Two or three

"Where two or three are gathered together in my name, there am I in the midst of them."

Matthew 18:20

Reflect on the things you love and are interested in: food, pleasures, hobbies. Relations and friends. Indulgences and entertainments. It would take you a long time to write them all down. Then there are all the different things you think about. You are full of multitudes of feelings and thoughts. Now, how many of these are friendly to Jesus? If there are only two or three, He is there in the midst. If you try to love Him and the neighbour, He is certainly present and will gradually bring all the things of your life into harmony and correspondence.

Prayer

Show me Your ways, O Lord; teach me Your paths, for You are the God of my salvation.

September 24

Rich man

"Then said Jesus to his disciples, Truly I say to you, that a rich man shall hardly enter into the kingdom of Heaven."

Matthew 19:23

A rich man! What does it mean?

There are rich men who are humble, kindly and generous: and there are poor men who are arrogant, rough and mean. In fact neither poverty nor riches make a man's character.

In Bible language a rich man represents one who is self-satisfied, proud and full of self-importance. It is hard indeed for such a man to enter into the kingdom of heaven. Before he can do so he must be converted and become as a little child.

Prayer

O Lord, I will rejoice in Your Word, as one that finds great spoil. Great peace have they who love Your law: and nothing shall offend them.

September 25

To be great

"Whoever will be great among you, let him be your minister; and whoever will be chief among you, let him be your servant."

>   Matthew 20:26, 27

To be great is to love. To be chief among men, is to serve. These qualities of love and service are the over-riding principles of true Christian life. Where these principles are acknowledged, and lived, people are happy and there is prosperity and contentment.

Insofar as you love God you want to serve Him, and just so far as you love your neighbour, you try to give him useful service. Those who love the Lord are great, and those who serve the neighbour are of chief importance.

Prayer

Lord, you have been our dwelling place in all generations, so teach us to number our days, that we apply our hearts unto wisdom.

September 26

The other side

"And the same day, when the evening came, He said to them, Let us pass over to the other side."

Mark 4:35

We often have to pass over to the other side. From one set of circumstances to another: for as we say, there are two sides to every question.

Spiritually it is the same. One side of our life is lived in outside natural things. The other side is lived among internal or spiritual things. Between the two positions there is a continual passing over, for the internal must bring the external part into harmony with itself. To this end there is interplay between the spiritual and natural positions.

When Jesus passes over with us all is well.

Prayer

O Lord, teach me good judgement and knowledge: for I have believed in Your commandments.

Daily Word

September 27

A storm

"And there arose a great storm of wind, and the waves beat into the ship, so that it was now full."

Mark 4:37

A great storm of wind! It represents the contrary weather we sometimes encounter on the sea of life; particularly when we pass over from an inner state to the things of bodily life.

The waves represent the mounting frustrations that arise from false ideas of life, and merely worldly concerns. And by their filling the ship, pictures our faith being almost swamped by them. Most of us experience storms of trouble like this, when we try to pass over to our outer life, the things we learn of the Lord.

Prayer

O Lord, when we cry to You in our trouble, bring us out of our distresses, and make the storm a calm, that the waves thereof be still.

Daily Word

September 28

Asleep

"And Jesus was in the rear part of the ship, asleep on a pillow: and they woke him, and said to Him, Master do you not care that we perish?"

Mark 4:38

Think of the ship as your faith, in, and by which you pass through life. Jesus is always with you inwardly in your faith; occasionally you are conscious of His presence, but often you are not. In this case the disciples had forgotten He was with them, and this is represented by His being asleep.

But when the storm breaks, their memory is aroused, and they cry out to Him for help. It was they who had for gotten Jesus, but now in fear they ask, "Care you not that we perish?"

Prayer

The floods have lifted up, O Lord, But You Lord, art mightier than the noise of many waters.

Daily Word

September 29

Peace

"And he arose, and rebuked the wind, and said to the sea, Peace, be still. And the wind ceased, and there was a great calm."

Mark 4:39

It happened long ago, but what matters so much is, that spiritually it happens now in our experiences: yours and mine.

By "He arose" is represented His presence in your mind in response to your cry for help. His words rebuking the wind, and telling the sea to be still, represent His ascendancy over your calamity. The wind ceasing, pictures the spirit of evil being driven back, and the great calm represents the peace Jesus gives to those who trust Him.

Prayer

We cry to You Lord, in our trouble, and You will bring us out of our distresses. O make, we pray You, the storm a calm, so that the waves thereof are still.

Daily Word

September 30

So fearful

"And he said to them, why are you so fearful? How is it that you have no faith?"

Mark 4:40

Why so fearful? It seems to be part of our heritage to be often frightened. So many things distress and upset us. How much happier we would be if all our fear could be taken away.

As our religious or spiritual life matures we do come into quieter experiences, and at last all our fearfulness will be left behind. It is a matter of faith. But true faith in Jesus can only grow as our love for Him grows. This is one reason why the first commandment is so important-you shall love the Lord your God with all your heart.

Prayer

O Lord God of hosts, who is a strong God like You? Or to Your faithfulness round about You?

Daily Word

October 1

Wind and sea

"And they feared exceedingly, and said one to another, What manner of man is this, that even the wind and the sea obey him?"

Mark 4:41

Even the wind and the sea obey him! This is surely almighty power: the disciples tremble in its presence. Yet all must obey the God of heaven and earth, or fall into destruction.
Here, the wind and sea represent the turbulent troubles and cares of worldly life. But when we allow the Lord to rule in our hearts and minds, all things of our lower life are brought into order. As we begin to realise His presence and power we are filled with wonder. What manner of man is this? It is God, in Divine humanity.

Prayer

Hear my prayer, O Lord, give ear to my supplications: in Your faithfulness answer me, and in Your righteousness.

October 2

Gadarenes

"And they came over to the other side of the sea, into the country of the Gadarenes."

Mark 5:1

The other side of the sea! The side bordering on the wilderness, opposite to the promised land.

Can you see this geography in your own person? The promised land is the heaven within. The other side, is your lower worldly life represented by the country of the Gadarenes.

Jesus and the disciples crossing over, is a picture of how Jesus comes with your affections for Him, from your inner mind, down into the common activities of your outer life. And this crossing over is in order that the things of your merely natural life may be brought into order and correspondence with spiritual principles.

Prayer

Out of the depths have I cried to You, O Lord. Hear the voice of my supplications.

Daily Word

October 3

An unclean spirit

"And when he was come out of the ship, immediately there met him out of the tombs a man with an unclean spirit."

Mark 5:2

A man out of the tombs! It is a strange picture. Think of it in relation to yourself. Directly Jesus steps out of your ship of faith, into your worldly and bodily appetites, there is a crisis. There must be, for two opposites are meeting.

The tombs represent dead things such as merely bodily pleasures. The spirit that dwells in them is unclean for it is entirely self-centred. It is difficult to appreciate the horrible nature of the uncleanness of self-love. But a little thought will show us how dead and tomb-like it is.

Prayer

Have mercy upon me O Lord, for I am in trouble: my strength fails because of my iniquity.

Daily Word

October 4

The tombs

"Who had his dwelling among the tombs, and no man could bind him, no, not with chains neither could any man tame him."

Mark 5:3, 4

A grim picture, and a sad one. A home among tombs: chains, and an ungovernable spirit.

Yet it may be a picture of ourselves, of you and me. Spiritually to dwell among tombs, is to live in the midst of evil indulgences-dying and dead things.

Not being able to be bound, not even with chains, represents the overpowering nature of the lusts of bodily life. They cannot be tamed by any man. But we need not despair for Jesus has come, and He knows how to save the lost.

Prayer

O Lord, I am forgotten as a dead man out of mind: I am like a broken vessel. But I trust in You, O Lord: You are my God.

Daily Word

October 5

Night and Day

"And always, night and day, he was in the mountains, and in the tombs, crying, and cutting himself with stones."

Mark 5:5

A picture of horror and misery!
Always, night and day, represents a state of alternating evil. In the mountain means, in the heights of self-love. The tombs signify dead delights. Crying, pictures misery, and cutting himself with stones, represents the hurt inflicted by false ideas and pursuits. This is a picture of deep distress, and a warning to us all. We must remember that though it may apply to only a small part of our bodily life-it is a deadly part. In the pleasures of self-love and self-indulgence there is nothing but death.

Prayer

My times are in Your hand, O Lord: deliver me from the hand of my enemies.

Daily Word

October 6

Jesus

"But when he saw Jesus afar off, he ran and worshipped him, and cried with a loud voice, and said, what have I to do with you, Jesus, you Son of the most high God? I adjure you by God, that you torment me not."

Mark 5:7

From states of evil depravity we see Jesus afar oft and urgently want to come to Him. But the evil within us is far removed from the Lord. It cannot have anything to do with Jesus; but He who came to save the lost has much to do with us.

But the love the Lord brings, is so different from our self-seeking love, that at first it torments us.

Prayer

O Lord, from the end of the earth will I cry to You, when my heart is overwhelmed: lead me to the rock that is higher than I.

Daily Word

October 7

Legion

"Jesus said to him, Come out of the man, you unclean spirit. And he asked him, what is your name? And he answered, saying, My name is Legion: for we are many."

          Mark 5:8, 9

Come out! This command of Jesus is to the unclean spirit, not to the man. For when evil goes out of us, good can enter.
First we must cease to do evil, then learn to do well. First repent, then heaven can enter. The name of the unclean spirit is Legion, because to every bad thing there are many others attached. Some are evident, others unseen but in unbroken sequence, like the links of a chain they are together from Hell. All evil is from hell: all good is from heaven.

Prayer

O You that hear prayer, unto You shall all flesh come.

Daily Word

October 8

The Swine

"And all the devils besought him, saying, Send us into the swine, that we may enter into them."

> Mark 5:12

This seems so strange. Why should the devils want to go into the swine?

All through life, like seeks like. Evil can only tolerate the company of evil. Similarly, good qualities can only dwell in the company of those who love and seek them. By the swine are represented unclean passions: these are the things devils seek. When we suffer the Lord to cast our lusts out, their devils go down into hell. And they go at their own request. Before the prodigal came to himself, he fed swine, but afterwards he left them, and returned to His father's home.

Prayer

Turn us again, O God, and cause Your face to shine; and we shall be saved.

Daily Word

October 9

They were choked

"And forthwith Jesus gave them leave, and the unclean spirits went out, and entered into the swine: and the herd ran violently down a steep place into the sea (they were about two thousand); and were choked in the sea.."

Mark 5:13

Jesus forces no man. We are free to follow Him or ourselves. When the unclean spirits left the man, the Lord gave them leave to do as they wished; which was that they might enter into the swine. The herd running violently down a steep place, represents the devil's eagerness for the company of hell here represented by the sea. By being choked is signified the suffocating nature of evil passions.

Prayer

Lord God of my salvation I have cried day and night before You. Let my prayer come before You: incline Your ear unto my cry.

Daily Word

October 10

They went to see

"And they that fed the swine fled, and told it in the city, and in the country. And they went out to see what it was that done."

Mark 5:14

They that fed the swine fled. They had no pigs to tend, they were all suffocated in the sea.

We are feeders of swine when we indulge our lusts, but when these leave us, so do the thoughts that cared for them. To tell it in the city and in the country is to let it be known in every part of our mind. The people coming out to see what had happened represents every lower thought we possess being made aware of the wonderful thing that has happened.

Prayer

Father, in heaven, I have sinned against Your sight, and am no more worthy to be called Your son.

Daily Word

October 11

Restored

"And they came to Jesus, and see him that was possessed with the devil, and had the legion, sitting, and clothed, and in his right mind: and they were afraid."

Mark 5:15

What a change! It is a picture of what can be done for a man who comes to Jesus. Not raving and cutting himself with stones now. But quietly sitting down, clothed and in his right mind.

When the devils go we rest in Jesus represented by sitting. Then we are clothed with habits and manners representing His teaching. Not maddened any more by fevers of self-love but in our right mind. It is a condition of rest after toil and of peace after storm.

Prayer

Let Your mercies come also to me, O Lord, even Your salvation, according to Your word.

Daily Word

October 12

A certain woman

"And a certain woman, which had an issue of blood twelve years, and had suffered many things of many physicians, and had spent all that she had, and was nothing bettered, but rather grew worse."

Mark 5:25, 26

It is about you. The woman represents your love of life, which is wasting away entirely. It is a spiritual disease. The physicians of the world only cause further suffering for they represent worldly indulgences: indulgences which, the world says, make life worth living, yet of themselves are deathlike.

To spend all that one has on these worldly pleasures, is to give them one's love and all one's thought: the result is a wasting disease.

Prayer

Be merciful to me, O Lord: for I cry unto You daily. Rejoice the soul of your servant: for to You, O Lord, do I lift up my soul.

Daily Word

October 13

Touch

"When she had heard of Jesus, came in behind, and touched his garment. For she said, If I may touch but his clothes, I shall be whole."

Mark 5:27, 28

Again, it is spiritually about you. Hearing of Jesus you want to come to Him. You know your life is wasting away: that you no longer find any satisfaction or delight in the way you live. To touch His clothes is to make contact with Him. His clothes represent His truth or teachings for these are the covering of His love. His truth, as He tells us, makes us free; free of disease and misery. Thus we become whole, and happy again.

Prayer

I cried to You, O Lord: I said, You are my refuge and my portion in the land of the living. Attend to my cry: for I am brought very low.

Daily Word

October 14

That plague

"And straightway the fountain of her blood was dried up; and she felt in her body that she was healed of that plague."

Mark 5:29

What a change! You humbly sought Jesus through the crowd of all the things that filled your mind. You touched His garments, that is, you contacted His wonderful truth, and drew it into your sick soul. Straightway you knew a great change had happened, life was worth living: it was no longer running away into a diseased melancholy. You felt new health in your body: the earthly receptacle of your soul was healed of the plague of dissipation and loss.

Prayer

O Lord, I asked You, deliver my soul. You have delivered my soul from death, my eyes from tears, and my feet from falling. I will walk before You, Lord, in the land of the living.

October 15

Fell down

"But the woman fearing and trembling, knowing what was done in her, came and fell down before him, and told him all the truth."

Mark 5:33

The woman, as we have said, represents our love of life. By fearing and trembling is understood holy fear and deep wonder at the marvellous change that has arisen. Before touching Jesus life was sad and miserable, now love and delight are alive again.

Falling down before Jesus signifies real repentance and humility. Telling Him all the truth pictures our readiness to open our hearts to Him. More really it represents our recognition that He knows all about us and is acquainted with all our ways.

Prayer

O Lord, remember not against us former iniquities: let Your tender mercies speedily prevent us: for we are brought very low.

Daily Word

October 16

Peace

"And he said to her, Daughter, your faith has made you whole; go in peace, and be whole of your plague."

Mark 5:34

It is a tender message, full of comfort. When our love is no longer wasted on self-indulgence, but humbly seeks the Lord, we become His children: His sons and daughters. The faith that makes us whole is our belief that He can heal and that causes us to make an effort to contact Him.

It is not what is called "faith alone" that heals, but faith which makes an active approach to touch Jesus. To be whole, is to be free from self-love-the one plague that wastes our lives.

Prayer

Help us, O God of our salvation, for the glory of Your name: and deliver us, and purge away our sins, for Your name's sake.

Daily Word

October 17

Devils

"And these signs shall follow them that believe: in my name they shall cast out devils; they shall speak with new tongues."

Mark 16:17

Signs of belief! But not signs that we are to look for in others, so much as signs in ourselves. The scriptures are for all, but the Lord is talking to you.

If your belief in Him is real, you will be casting out devils! Not out of others but out of yourself. First cast out the beam from your own eye, as Jesus teaches. The devils are the desires of selfish gain and selfish pleasures, and their self-seeking acquaintances.

To speak with new tongues is the next sign. Not new languages, but new intelligence, new love and kindness, the teaching of Jesus.

Prayer

In You, O Lord, do I put my trust: let me never be put to confusion.

Daily Word

October 18

Serpents

"They shall take up serpents; and if they drink any deadly thing, it shall not hurt them."

Mark 16:18

Serpents! Why should one who believes in Jesus pick them up? It is because serpents spiritually represent the things of the senses. The senses particularly of natural life that are cunning and deceiving. When we believe in Jesus we lift our natural life and all its senses on to a higher plane.

Drinking deadly things means hearing and perhaps imbibing false ideas and teachings. To some extent we all do, or have done, this. But again, belief in Jesus removes the harm, for His truth becomes our standard and frees us from harm.

Prayer

O Lord, let Your tender mercies come to me, that I may live: for Your law is my delight. Let my heart be sound in Your statutes.

October 19

The sick

"And they shall lay their hands on the sick, and they shall recover."

Mark 16:18

How very wonderful to be able to do this. Would you like to have such ability? If you can believe in the risen Jesus you can do it. Indeed it is one of the signs of your belief.

There is just one person in this world whom you can recover from this kind of sickness. It is yourself! In the Name of Jesus, and from your belief in Him, you can lay your hands on the spiritual sickness of your affections and thoughts till they recover. Till instead of loving yourself first, you love Jesus first, and think of His kingdom in all your propositions.

To lay on your hands represents applying your strength from the Lord.

Prayer

Let Your mercies come also unto me, O Lord, even Your salvation, according to Your word.

October 20

Martha

"And it came to pass as they went, that he entered into a certain village: and a certain woman named Martha received him into her house."

Luke 10:38

It is the beginning of a much loved story. But try to think of it as relating to yourself. Jesus enters into a little part of your faith, represented by the village. You appreciate His presence, and welcome Him into your house, which spiritually is your mind. Martha, being a woman, represents your feeling or affection for Jesus. But it is a mental affection, rather than an affection of the heart. In tomorrow's reading you will see the difference in the representation of Martha and her sister.

Prayer

O God, You are my God: early will I seek You: my soul thirsts for You, my flesh longs for You.

October 21

Mary

"And she had a sister called Mary, which also sat at Jesus' feet, and heard his word."

Luke 10:39

Martha had a sister called Mary. Martha represents your mental affection for Jesus as previously stated. But together with the affection of your mind is a sister affection represented by Mary.

Now Mary is an affection of the heart, represented by her sitting at the feet of Jesus: also by her listening to His Word which reveals a state of humility which is always present when we truly love the Lord.

To sit at the feet of Jesus is to subject ourselves to His providence in all things of our life.

Prayer

I remembered Your name, O Lord, in the night, and have kept Your law. You are my portion, O Lord: I have said that I would keep Your words.

Daily Word

October 22

Serve alone

"But Martha was cumbered about much serving, and came to him, and said, Lord, do You not care that my sister has left me to serve alone? Therefore ask that she help me."

Luke 10:40

Martha is much cumbered! She, you will remember, signifies the part of our mind that does the thinking. Its part is to serve the loving side of life by planning and providing. Sometimes 'I' forgets it is the servant of love, then it complains. Must I serve alone, it asks? It is an appearance that the thinking comes first and does all the work. Actually, thinking is only the executive of loving. When love for Jesus fails, thinking of Him ceases.

Prayer

O God, You have taught me from my youth: and hitherto have I declared Your wondrous works.

October 23

Troubled

"Jesus answered and said to her, Martha, Martha, you are careful and troubled about many things: but one thing is needful and Mary has chosen that good part, which shall not be taken away from her."

Luke 10:41, 42

The mind often becomes troubled and perplexed. It has much to do and many problems to handle. It can only be at rest when it acts from love for the Lord. The one needful thing, the good part for a quiet mind, is beautifully represented by Mary.

As soon as we give our love to the Lord and listen to His Word, our Martha part, representing our mental affection, is quietened and we become happy.

Prayer

Your hands have made me, O Lord, and fashioned me: give me understanding, that I may learn Your commandments. And let Your merciful kindness be for my comfort.

Daily Word

October 24

Begging

"And it came to pass, that as He came close to Jericho, a certain blind man sat by the wayside begging. And hearing the multitudes pass by, he asked what it meant. And they told him that Jesus of Nazareth passed by."

Luke 18:35-37

Jericho is at the foot of the hills where the road goes up to Jerusalem. Jericho represents knowledge of the Lord through which we pass to the spiritual Jerusalem, the Holy City, representing the church and heaven.

Like the blind man we sit by the wayside begging till Jesus comes, or until we realise His presence. Then if we are poor in spirit we beg Him to help us.

Prayer

Out of the depths have I cried to You, O Lord. Lord hear my voice: let Your ears be attentive to the voice of my supplications.

Daily Word

October 25

He cried

"And he cried, saying, Jesus, you son of David, have mercy on me. And Jesus stood, and commanded him to be brought to Him."

Luke 18:38, 40

It is the cry of desperate need. The prayer of a blind beggar. If you are able to say, "It represents me", you are blessed indeed. The Lord can help the broken, and poor in spirit. For this poor man, the kingdom of heaven is at hand!

By, "Jesus stood" is signified the Lord's presence: by asking for the beggar to be brought to Jesus, is signified, the inducement of all the man's thoughts to help him. The man has cried vehemently for mercy, and mercy is now about to enter into his very being.

Prayer

Lord, I will praise You: for You has heard me, and art become my salvation.

Daily Word

October 26

My sight

"And when he was come near, he asked him, saying what will you that I shall do to you? And he said, Lord, that I may receive my sight."

Luke 18:40, 41

What a question! And what an opportunity for the blind man. When he was come near, represents our spiritual approach to the Lord. As we draw near we realise how urgent Jesus is to help us. And we answer His wonderful question directly, "Lord, that I may receive my sight."

The physical blindness of the beggar corresponds, of course, to our spiritual blindness. Somehow, we have found it difficult to believe: the eyes of our understanding have been closed, but now, by the wayside, is this great opportunity.

Prayer

And now, Lord, what wait I for? my hope is in You. Deliver me from all my transgressions.

Daily Word

October 27

Saved!

"And Jesus said to him, Receive your sight: your faith has saved you. And immediately he received his sight, and followed Jesus, glorifying God: and all the people, when they saw it, gave praise to God."

Luke 18:42, 43

Receive your sight! How wonderful it must have been for the beggar. It can be even more wonderful for you. For the beggar in the story it was physical sight; for you it can be spiritual sight. The day your eyes are opened to see Jesus will be one of the greatest of your life. If you cry out to Jesus as this man of Jericho did, trusting Him for deliverance, your faith in Jesus will open your eyes. Always afterwards you will follow Him.

Prayer

In You, O Lord, do I put my trust: deliver me in Your righteousness.

Daily Word

October 28

Light

"That was the true Light, which lights every man that comes into the world."

John 1:9

It refers to Jesus, the Light of life. Without light we could not see anything in the world about us. Similarly, without spiritual light the eyes of the mind cannot see any thing in the spiritual sphere. to Jesus is the true light; from Him comes all the light of our understandings. The more we love Him, the more light we have, for all light arises from love. Even in the natural world, the more we love it the more beauty we see.

Jesus has told us that they who follow Him shall not walk in darkness, but shall have the light of life.

Prayer

O Lord, You are my light and my salvation: whom shall I fear? You are the strength of my life, of whom shall I be afraid?

October 29

The World

"He was in the world, and the world was made by him, and the world knew him not."

John 1:10

It is speaking of Jesus: Immanuel, God with us. Present with us in the world He made, but unrecognised and unknown. Similarly, He is in the world of your life today. In the busy world of your mind, with its teeming feelings and thoughts. The little world of your own, made especially for you: where the sun of love rises and sets, and where the winds of your spirit blow.

But although He is present in your world, do you know Him? He is present to bring you love and understanding: to heal your sickness and disease: to save you from yourself.

Prayer

Create in me a clean heart, O God; and renew a right spirit within me.

Daily Word

October 30

Born again

"Marvel not that I said unto you, Ye must be born again."

John 3:7

The truth is that the will of man is so depraved by the love of itself, that without a new beginning, we could have no hope of reaching heaven. Our first birth is of the earth, and for first purposes. Our new birth must be of the spirit, and for spiritual purposes.

To this end our mind must be lighted by the lamp of truth, which truth comes to us as we read the Lord's Word.

By this means the holy seed is sown into our hearts, and from this holy spiritual seed new life begins. Thus, by the mysterious, secret workings of providence we are born again.

Prayer

Behold, God is my salvation: I will trust, and not be afraid.

Daily Word

October 31

The Wind

"The wind blows where it wants, and you hear the sound thereof, but cannot tell from where it comes, nor where it goes: so is every one that is born of the Spirit."

John 3:8

The wind blows! It is often tiresome, but it is a great cleanser. It represents the spirit of truth. It blows through our minds without our bidding, and we know not whence it comes or whither it goes. It may visit us as a gentle breeze or a whirling storm. It stirs up our understanding and often cleanses our thinking. Our new birth comes too, like the spirit of truth. We know not how, nor anything of its beginning, any more than we do of the first days of our natural birth.

Prayer

Behold, Lord, I have longed after Your precepts: quicken me in Your righteousness.

November 1

Drink

"There comes a woman of Samaria to draw water: Jesus says to her, Give me to drink."

John 4:7

Jesus asks for a drink! But the woman questions His request. He is a Jew she is a Samaritan.

A woman of Samaria represents a desire of the mind. Coming to draw water represents seeking truth. Jesus asking her for a drink represents the Lord's need of our mind's affections.

Samaria represents the affection of truth and Jerusalem the affection of good. Jesus asking for a drink of the Samaritan woman really signifies His desire that the affection of truth be conjoined with the affection of good. Truth without love is not really alive.

Prayer

Be merciful to me, O Lord: for I cry to You daily. Rejoice the soul of Your servant; for unto You, O Lord, do I lift up my soul.

November 2

Living Water

"Jesus answered and said to her, If you knew the gift of God, and who it is that says to you, Give me to drink; you would have asked of Him, and He would have given you living water."

John 4:10

The gift of God! It is the gift of living water. Living water is God's truth arising from His love. When we drink truth alone we thirst again, but when truth is infilled with love it really does quench our thirst. To ask Jesus for this living water is very different from drawing water ourselves out of the wells of the earth. So ask Jesus for it, He says, "If any man thirst let him come unto me and drink."

Prayer

As the hart longs after the water brooks, so my soul pants after You, O God.

November 3

Rise up

"Jesus says to him, Rise, take up your bed, and walk."

John 5:8

The man is sick, but Jesus tells him to get up and walk! It concerned this man of Jerusalem, but it also concerns you. The man was impotent, and represents all who are spiritually sick. The bed on which he lay corresponds to doctrine, or shall we say, one's faith. When we are physically sick we lie down on a natural bed, but when spiritually sick we rest in our faith or spiritual bed.

But we must not rest too long; we cannot live by faith alone. To take up our bed and walk at the command of Jesus, is to live the life of faith. When we do this our health is restored.

Prayer

I know, O Lord, that Your judgements are right: let Your tender mercies come unto me.

Daily Word

November 4

Bread

"Jesus said to them, I am the bread of life: he that comes to me shall never hunger; and he that believes on me shall never thirst."

John 6:35

Jesus is the bread of life.
Notice the word, life. This is not referring to the body which of itself is dead. It is to do with the life within, which animates the body by infilling the spirit, the real man in the body.

Just as the body feeds on natural bread, so the spirit feeds on spiritual bread, which is the love that is Jesus. And to believe in Him, is never to thirst, for He is the truth. To come to Jesus is to love Him. To believe on Him is to keep His sayings.

Prayer

Our Father, give us this day our daily bread.

November 5

Eternal life

"Whoever eats my flesh, and drinks my blood, has eternal life; and I will raise him up at the last day."

John 6:54

To eat the flesh of Jesus is to feed on the goodness of His love. We can do this by learning to love both what He loves and what He teaches.

To drink the blood of Jesus is to absorb His truth, which is revealed in His Word; and then to regulate our thinking and activities by its requirements.

If we do this our spiritual life will be warmed by His love, and lighted by His truth. This will introduce us to eternal life, and at the end of our trials we shall be raised up to Him.

Prayer

Bow down Your ear, O Lord, hear me: for I am poor and needy. For great is Your mercy toward me.

Daily Word

November 6

Spirit and Life

"It is the spirit that gives life; the flesh profits nothing: the words that I speak to you, they are spirit and they are life."

John 6:63

The flesh apart from the spirit is dead. It is the spirit of life from the Lord that quickens, and enables us to live. It is very similar with the Lord's Word, it is the spirit within that gives it life.

The words the Lord speaks are spirit and are life, because the spirit represents His divine truth, and the life represents His divine love. And His truth and love are everywhere present in the Word. The words without the spirit are dead.

Prayer

Lord, my soul clings unto the dust: keep me according to Your word. My soul melts for heaviness; strengthen You me according unto Your word.

Daily Word

November 7

Verily!

"Most assuredly, I say to you, If a man keeps my saying, he shall never see death."

John 8:51

The Lord's sayings! To keep them is to live for ever! Verily, verily means absolute certainty. To keep the Lord's word signifies a honour and respect in the mind, and compliance to its standards in the activities of life.

His word is essential truth, and it is infilled with divine love: to keep it is to live from Him. And to live from Him is to be conjoined with Him, and this in turn is eternal life. Life which never sees death. The earthly body must die, but the soul inhabiting it will live for ever. Nothing conjoined with the Lord can die.

Prayer

Hear my cry, O God; attend to my prayer. From the end of the earth will I cry to You, when my heart is overwhelmed lead me to the rock that is higher than I.

Daily Word

November 8

The door

"I am the door: by me if any man enter in, he shall be saved, and shall go in and out, and shall find pasture."

John 10:9

The door! The entrance to eternal life and all happiness. The door represents the way and the truth, that introduce us to our Father's love, and so our Father Himself.

To enter life through this door is to be saved from the miseries of self-seeking; and from worldly pleasures that successively die. To go in and out of this door, is to find pasture for our souls; the food and delight of love and wisdom, for ever. "Any man" means, of course, all of us - you and me!

Prayer

Withhold not You Your tender mercies from me, O Lord: let your loving kindness and Your truth continually preserve me.

Daily Word

November 9

My sheep

"My sheep hear my voice, and I know them, and they follow me: and I give to them eternal life."

John 10:27, 28

The Lord's sheep represent His people, those who hear His voice and follow Him. The Lord knows them individually, all their weaknesses and frailties and their peculiar need every moment. He knows you!

His sheep follow Him, that is, they hear His voice in His Word, and live by His sayings. And He gives them eternal life. If you follow Him He will give you eternal life. He will prepare a home for you in heaven, where to grow old is to grow young. Your cup will run over and you will dwell in the house of the Lord for ever.

Prayer

Yea, Lord, though I walk through the valley of the shadow of death I will fear no evil.

November 10

Believe

"I am the resurrection, and the life: he that believes in me, though he were dead yet shall he live."

John 11:25

He that believes! What a wonderful thing believing is. If we believe in self as of first importance, self destroys us. If on the other hand, we believe in Jesus, He gives us life that can never die.

Even though one dies as to worldly life, if he believes in Jesus, he is raised up and lives. Belief does this, because it attaches us to what we believe. And to be attached to Jesus is to be conjoined with the resurrection and the life. All things are possible to him that believes.

Prayer

O Lord, open to me the gates of righteousness: I will go into them, and I will praise the Lord.

Daily Word

November 11

Odour of ointment

"Then took Mary a pound of ointment of spikenard, very costly, and anointed the feet of Jesus, and wiped his feet with her hair: and the house was filled with the odour of the ointment."

John 12:3

It is a picture of loving kindness; and what it can do for one's house, which signifies both the natural and rational minds.

The ointment, very costly, represents love. The feet of Jesus represent His love for us, in human form. The house, as aid, signifies the mind-yours or mine. When we welcome Jesus into the house of the mind and begin to love His least teachings, then our least thoughts are applied to His needs. Our love thus expanded on Him, receives His love, and the house of our mind is filled with its fragrance.

Prayer

O Lord, open You my eyes that I may behold wondrous things out of Your law.

Daily Word

November 12

New Commandment

"A new commandment I give unto you, that ye love one another; as I have loved you, that ye also love one another. By this shall all men know that ye are my disciples."

John 13:34, 35

A new commandment, but it comprises all the others. It is so simple, yet so profound. Just that we love one another even as Jesus loves us. And He loves us always, and in all circumstances; especially seeking us when we are broken and lost.

Even when He rebukes and chastens us it is that we may be brought from misery into happiness. Receiving such wonderful love ourselves, we are to pass it on to others. It is the one sign that we really are disciples of Jesus.

Prayer

Great are Your tender mercies, O Lord: keep me according to Your judgements.

November 13

The Father

"Jesus says to him, Have I been so long time with you, and yet have you not known me, Philip? He that has seen me has seen the Father; and how can you say, show us the Father?

John 14:9

So long time! Have you known the name of Jesus a long time? Perhaps from early childhood in your old home? Many of us have. He has been with you always, even from the very beginning. For without Him you can do nothing.

If at times you have loved Him only a little, you have seen Him in your mind. He is your heavenly Father come to seek and save you. If you seek Him and love Him you will see He is your Father.

Prayer

In You, O Lord do I put my trust: let me never be put to confusion.

Daily Word

November 14

If!

"If ye keep my commandments, ye shall abide in my love."

John 15:10

If! Always there are conditions. It is a mistake to think we can have the costly blessings of spiritual life unconditionally, we cannot!

We can abide in the Lord's love if we keep His commandments. And what a wonderful home to abide in: a home where all is love, always. Where we can go in and out and find pasture. Where we can find every comfort and divine understanding in all circumstances.

And the commandments themselves express love in practice. Love for the Lord, the God of love, and love for one another. What kind of living could be happier?

Prayer

Consider how I love Your precepts: keep me, O Lord, according to Your loving kindness. Your word is true from the beginning. I rejoice in Your word as one that finds great spoil.

Daily Word

November 15

Friends

"Greater love has no man than this, that a man lay down his life for his friends. Ye are my friends, if ye do whatsoever I command you."

John 15:13, 14

Laying down life! What does it mean? It means what it says, but it says more than is often appreciated. It may mean sometimes laying down bodily life for another. But it always means laying down the life of self, and self-seeking, for the life of service to others.

And we become friends of Jesus, when we lay down our will for His will. When from our hearts we pray-"Your will be done."

There is no greater love than this. But it makes us friends of Jesus.

Prayer

Our Father: Your kingdom come, Your will be done, as in heaven, so upon the earth.

Daily Word

November 16

The Title

"And Pilate wrote a title, and put it on the cross. And the writing was, JESUS OF NAZARETH THE KING OF THE JEWS."

John 19:19

The Title! Only twice is Jesus given the title of King of the Jews. Once at the time of His birth and again at the time of His death.

The name Jesus represents Divine love, and by King is represented truth or Divine wisdom.

This inscription over the cross as related to ourselves represents His love ruling in our hearts and deeds and His truth ruling in our understandings and thence in our words. The cross represents the denial or sacrifice of the self in us.

Prayer

Out of the depths have I cried unto You, O Lord. Lord, hear my voice: let Your ears be attentive to the voice of my supplications.

November 17

The garden

"In the place where Jesus was crucified there was a garden; and in the garden a new sepulchre, wherein was never a man yet laid. There laid they Jesus."

John 19:41

In the place where Jesus was crucified there was a garden. From the place of the skull, the emblem of death, where the cross was set up, to the garden, the bright emblem of life, where the sepulchre was carved, and where the resurrection took place, was but a step. In the garden, near to the cross, there was a new sepulchre, how significant. The sepulchre represents resurrection."

It was new, where no man had laid, representing the great truth that the Lord was the first in whom humanity was made new.

Prayer

Our Father, deliver us from evil. For your is the kingdom, and the power, and the glory for ever. Amen.

Daily Word

November 18

Angels

"Mary stood without at the sepulchre weeping: and as she wept, she stooped down, and looked into the sepulchre. And saw two angels in white sitting the one at the head, and the other at the feet, where the body of Jesus had lain."

John 20:11, 12

The angels were the first to tell Mary, and through Mary the church, that the Lord had risen.

In relation to us the angels represent God's messages of truth enlightening our minds. Mary represents the church and, in particular, the church in us. Mary stooping down and weeping, signifies deep sorrow that we have seemingly lost the Lord, while we feel such a need for His love.

Prayer

O Lord, let all those that seek You rejoice and be glad in You: let such as love Your salvation say continually, the Lord be magnified.

Daily Word

November 19

Mary

"Jesus says to her, Mary. She turned herself, and says to him, Rabboni: which is to say, Master. Mary Magdalene came and told the disciples she had seen the Lord."

John 20:16, 18

When Jesus speaks to us by name, as He did to Mary, it shows how well He knows us. Spiritually one's name is a picture of one's quality. Jesus knows one's quality absolutely, every feeling and every thought. Mary turning and saying, Master, represents the church within us recognising Him as our teacher. And her coming and telling the disciples she has seen the Lord represents our acknowledgement that this Master or teacher is our Lord and Saviour in human form.

Prayer

Search me, O God, and know my heart: try me and know my thoughts: and see if there be any wicked way in me, and lead me in the way everlasting.

Daily Word

November 20

Peace

"The same day at evening, being the first day of the week, when the doors were shut where the disciples were assembled for fear of the Jews, came Jesus and stood in the midst, and says to them, Peace be to you."

John 20:19

"**In** the evening time there shall be light." The Light itself stood in their midst. It is the evening of the first day of the week. The beginning of a new experience, for Jesus is risen. The doors being shut represents being closed against all disturbances of the mind. It is then that Jesus enters into our midst, and we see Him with our mind's eye. Thus the Prince of peace passes to us, joining all our love for Him with our thinking, taking away all discord.

Prayer

Lord, give ear to my voice, when I cry unto You.

Daily Word

November 21

The right side

"Jesus said to them, Cast the net on the right side of the ship, and you shall find. They cast therefore, and now they were not able to draw it for the multitude of fishes."

John 21:6

The right side of the ship! Your ship is your doctrine or your faith. The right side is the good side, and the left side is the truth side. The net represents your affections which do all the fishing. But it is necessary to fish from the good, or love side of your faith. Then like the disciples of long ago you will find your net full to overflowing. Truth keeps your faith on its course, but love lifts the harvest.

Prayer

Remember me, O Lord, with the favour that You hear Your people: O visit me with Your salvation.

Daily Word

November 22

Feed my sheep

"He says to him the third time, Simon, son of Jonas, do you love me? Peter was grieved because he said to him the third time, Do you love me? And he said to him, Lord, you know all things; you know that I love you. Jesus says to him, Feed my sheep."

John 21:17

Three times Jesus asked Peter if he loved Him. Peter represents truth, the rock on which the Lord builds His church.
In you too, the Lord builds His church on the rock of His truth. It is important that you love His truth. You do, if you love Him. The question: "Love you me?" concerns you. If your answer be "you know that I love you" then Jesus says, "Feed my sheep."
His sheep are all good thoughts that follow Him.

Prayer

Lord, lead me in the paths of righteousness.

Daily Word

November 23

Wretched

"Because you say, I am rich, and increased with goods, and have need of nothing: and knows not that you are wretched, and miserable, and poor, and blind, and naked."

Revelation 3:17

Sometimes we think we are rich, and have need of nothing. As yet we do not see that worldly riches fall away, and that spiritual riches endure.

We are wretched when we have no spiritual abiding place: and miserable when we have no truth, and poor indeed when we are without good from the Lord. And we are blind and naked, when we cannot see truth, nor clothe our selves with its teaching. In the following verse the Lord tells us how to acquire spiritual wealth.

Prayer

Withhold not You Your tender mercies from me, O Lord: let Your loving kindness and Your truth continually preserve me.

November 24

Chastening

"As many as I love, I rebuke and chasten: be zealous therefore, and repent."

Revelation 3:19

When we are troubled and tempted by falsity, it seems that the Lord is rebuking us. And when indulgence in selfish desires results in pain and misery, we feel it is the chastening of the Lord. Actually it results from our own folly, for directly we suffer ourselves to be led by Him we come into happy states.

It is because the Lord loves us that He allows the rebuking and chastening, for these may lead us to repentance: and repentance opens the door to heaven, and all happiness. To be zealous, is to be serious and urgent in our efforts to turn from self to the Lord.

Prayer

Consider how I love Your precepts: keep me, O Lord, according to Your loving kindness.

November 25

The door

"Behold, I stand at the door, and knock:' if any man hear my voice, and open the door, I will come in to him, and I'll sup with him, and he with me."

> Revelation 3:20

The Bible is like a door. A very wonderful door, opening outwards into the natural world and inwards into the spiritual world. It is here that the Lord stands urgent to be received. To hear His voice is to hear Him speaking to us in His Word; and we open the door to Him, when we do as He teaches. Then He comes not only to us, but into us, by entering into our affections and into our thinking. Then we sup together He with us and we with Him.

Prayer

O Lord, let Your word be a lamp unto my feet, and a light unto my path.

November 26

Many angels

"And I beheld, and I heard the voice of many angels round about the throne and the beasts and the elders: and the number of them was ten thousand times ten thousand, and thousands of thousands."

Revelation 5:11

It is a picture of the people of the heavens. Round about the throne represents their humiliation and adoration of the Lord,
Who is the centre of all their doings. and delights. Their number pictures the whole multitude of angels, and represents not so much numbers as we count people, but the infinite range of the qualities of love and wisdom from which the Lord is praised.
You may be numbered even now with these happy people.

Prayer

Cause me to hear Your loving kindness in the morning, O Lord, for in You do I trust: I lift up my soul unto You.

November 27

Glory

"Saying, Amen: Blessing, and glory, and wisdom, and thanksgiving, and honour, and power, and might, be to our God for ever and ever. Amen."

Revelation 7:12

Amen signifies Divine Truth, and confirmation from it. Blessing, and glory, and wisdom, and thanksgiving signify the Divine Spiritual attributes of the Lord. But honour, and power, and might, signify the highest qualities of all, that are called Celestial. By, be unto our God for ever and ever, signifies that these attributes of the Lord are eternal, and to all eternity.

Amen, signifies again Divine Truth, and its confirmation by all who love the Lord and live in His ways.

Prayer

Let Your hand help me; for I have chosen Your precepts, O Lord. I have longed for Your salvation, O Lord; and Your law is my delight. Let my soul live, and it shall praise You.

Daily Word

November 28

White robes

"These are they that came out of great tribulation, and have washed their robes, and made them white in the blood of the Lamb."

Revelation 7:14

Great tribulation is part of the cost of our regeneration. It results from the evils of self-love, and false thinking, fighting against us as we try to love the Lord and our neighbour.

We wash our robes and make them white, as we apply the teaching of the Lord's Word to our daily activities. White robes signify principles made pure by truth. And to wash them in the Lord's blood, represents cleansing them in the Divine Truth of the Lord's Divine Love.

Prayer

O Lord, before I was afflicted I went astray: but now I have kept Your word. You are good, and do good: teach me Your statutes.

November 29

The Lamb

"They shall hunger no more, neither thirst any more; neither shall the sun light on them, nor any heat. For the Lamb which is in the midst of the throne shall feed them, and shall lead them to living fountains of waters: and God shall wipe away all tears from their eyes."

Revelation 7: 16, 17

Being in the presence of God, we never hunger nor thirst, for He feeds us with the bread and water of His love and wisdom.
We are no longer troubled by evil desires or false persuasions. The Lord alone, represented by the Lamb, cares for all our needs, and is ever in the midst. By wiping tears from our eyes, signifies the end of all trials and temptations.

Prayer

Unto You, do I lift up my eyes, O You that dwells in the heavens.

November 30

First and Last

"I am the Alpha and Omega, the beginning and the end, the first and the last."

Revelation 22:13

The Lord is all in all. Wonderful, and Prince of Peace. He is Jesus the first and the last. He is King of Kings, and Lord of Lords. He is Immanuel, God with us. He is the Lamb in the midst of the throne. To see Him is to see our Heavenly Father. To hear Him speaking to us is to hear our Father's voice. To love Him is to love all others. To live for Him is to live in eternal happiness. He is Alpha and Omega, the beginning and the end, the first and the last.

Prayer

Lord, I cry to You: make haste to me; give ear to my voice, when I cry to You.

December 1

A child

"For unto us a child is born, unto us a son is given: and the government shall be on his shoulder."

Isaiah 9:6

This was written long before Jesus came, even hundreds of years. And yet, it is in the present tense. You see, it refers to us all: to the people of long ago, and to you and me today.

Jesus was born into the world; and is born into the world of our minds, just as the prophecy says. He came to seek and save the lost, and He comes to your own personal world, and mine, for the same reason. He is the truth given to us from Heaven, to take over the government of our minds.

Prayer

O Lord, Your hands have made me and fashioned me: give me understanding, that I may learn Your commandments.

December 2

Jesus

"Now when Jesus was born in Bethlehem of Judaea in the days of Herod the king, behold, there came wise men from the east to Jerusalem."

Matthew 2:1

Bethlehem of Judaea. In relation to yourself, Bethlehem of Judaea represents the church, or your religious life. It is that part of you, where you love to do what you see is right.

This is where Jesus is born, eventually to enter into the whole world of your daily life. In the days of Herod the King, represents in states of selfish control. Wise men, signify good thoughts. Coming from the east, means from the Lord. Thus the Lord provides, and leads us to Himself.

Prayer

O Lord, from the end of the earth will I cry unto You, when my heart is overwhelmed: lead me to the rock that is higher than I.

Daily Word

December 3

Where?

"Saying, Where is he that is born King of the Jews? for we have seen his star in the east, and are come to worship him."

Matthew 2:2

Where is He? They that seek, find!
Jesus being spoken of as the King of the Jews, represents His government of Divine Truth. Seeing His star in the east, represents for us, seeing His truth shining from His love.

Coming to worship Him represents our acknowledgement of Him as our Lord, and our desire to come to Him. But at first, though we have seen the light, we are not sure of the way to find Him. So we continue to seek and enquire.

Prayer

O God, You are my God; early will I seek You: my soul thirsts for You, my flesh longs for You in a dry and thirsty land without water.

Daily Word

December 4

Herod

"When Herod the king had heard these things, he was troubled, and all Jerusalem with him."

Matthew 2:3

Herod was troubled! In such circumstances he always is. He represents evil government, both in the world about us, and in the little world of our own souls. Self-love does not want to be ruled by love for God, or by love for the neighbour. When it is conscious of wise men, or of God's truths within us, disturbing his kingship he is troubled. And all Jerusalem, here representing our false religious life, is troubled as well.

We can accept Herod and his rule, or we can seek God and His government. The choice is ours.

Prayer

O Lord, happy is he that has the God of Jacob for his help, whose hope is in the Lord his God, which made heaven and earth.

December 5

What time?

"Then Herod, when he had privily called the wise men, enquired of them diligently what time the star appeared."

Matthew 2:7

Herod does his enquiring privately. Like selfish love he is cunning.

We are in the same position when we seek the truth for our own ends, that it may serve self. He enquires diligently; it is important to Herod that this new king be discovered and overcome. What time did the star appear? or spiritually understood, in what state of life were we, to see this truth of Jesus?

Just as there are wise men in the world, so there are wise thoughts in our hearts. We do well to be guided by them.

Prayer

Unto You, O Lord, will I sing. I will behave myself wisely in a perfect way. O when will You come to me?

Daily Word

December 6

The Star

"When they had heard the king, they departed: and, behold, the star, which they saw in the east, went before them, till it came and stood over where the young child was."

Matthew 2:9

The wise men now leave the king. In the world of our minds we leave King Herod when we turn away from our selfish reasoning. And when we depart, then the star appears again. We could not see it while in the presence of Herod.

By the star going before us is represented our following the truth revealed to us from heaven. This truth stands over the place where Jesus is in our minds just, as long ago, it did at Bethlehem in the world outside of us.

Prayer

Lord, so teach us to number our days, that we may apply our hearts to wisdom.

Daily Word

December 7

Great joy

"When they saw the star, they rejoiced with exceeding great joy."

Matthew 2:10

Exceeding great joy! This picture of the wise men rejoicing has had a distinctive place in the Christmas story, down through the ages. And how true it is in our spiritual experience. Herod the king, and all he represents, blinds our eyes to the star. While we are with him we lose its light, and its guiding: but when we leave our self-seeking we find it again. Then we are happy, and our rejoicing can hardly be over-expressed.

The star of truth guides us to Jesus, Who is Himself the Bright and Morning Star of all our hope and peace.

Prayer

Cause me to hear Your loving kindness in the morning, O Lord, for in You do I trust: and cause me to know the way wherein I should walk.

Daily Word

December 8

In the house

"And when they were come into the house, they saw the young child with Mary his mother, and fell down and worshipped him."

Matthew 2:11

The wise men came into the house. The house represents, spiritually, your mind.
When wise thoughts enter fully into you, then you clearly see Jesus. Mary represents the church or, shall we say, the faith of your religious principles. When you see Jesus like this you love Him. To fall down and worship Him, is a picture of humility in His presence. True worship is always from a humble heart.

To open the door of the house of the mind to wise thoughts from Jesus is to find delight of life.

Prayer

I have longed for Your salvation, O Lord; and Your law is my delight. Let my soul live and it shall praise You.

Daily Word

December 9

Gifts

"And when they had opened their treasures, they presented to him gifts: gold, and frankincense, and myrrh."

Matthew 2:11

Treasures! All our treasures are of the heart.

The things we love most are treasured most. The wise men opening their treasures represent you opening your heart before Jesus, that is, if you are numbered with the wise. The three gifts from your treasures are the most costly of all. There is nothing you can give of more value than these.

The first is Gold representing your love. The second Frankincense, representing your thinking of Him, or your faith. And the third, Myrrh, represents your love for the Lord together with your faith in active obedience to His will.

Prayer

Bless the Lord, O my soul. O Lord my God, You are very great; You are clothed with honour and majesty.

Daily Word

December 10

Another way

"And being warned by God in a dream that they should not return to Herod, they departed into their own country another way."

Matthew 2:12

The warning! When once we have seen Jesus and given Him our love, we must not return to Herod: remember! Herod is evil and represents the love of self. We must now return to our own country; our own kind of life; another way. We found Jesus by the guiding star of truth, it led us from Jerusalem to His birth place. Having opened our hearts to Him, we return not by truth, but by the way of love. Henceforth, Jesus is the Sun of our souls.

Prayer

O Lord, truly I am Your servant: You have loosed my bonds, I will offer to You the sacrifice of thanksgiving, and will call upon Your name.

December 11

To Egypt

"When he arose, he took the young child and his mother by night, and departed into Egypt."

Matthew 2:14

On our first finding Jesus, and offering Him our love, we are filled with jubilation. But soon afterwards we often come into difficulties. Our spiritual state seems to be darkened, which is here represented by the child being taken by night.

We all have to take our love for Jesus down into Egypt-that is down into the natural things of daily life. In this kind of life things are so busy, that we seem to forget Him. But while with us still, He is as it were hidden, and safe from the destroying nature of self-love-the Herod of our souls.

Prayer

Out of the depths have I cried unto You, O Lord, Lord, hear my voice.

December 12

Jesus

"And the angel said to her, Fear not, Mary: for you have found favour with God. And, behold, you shall conceive in your womb, and bring forth a son, and shall call his name Jesus."

Luke 1:30, 31

This of course is true history, and full of wonder. But in relation to ourselves it represents the coming of Jesus to us.
We find favour with God when we receive the faith of Jesus into our lives. The angel represents a message from heaven telling us of this. To bring forth a son pictures the birth of the Lord's truth into our minds. Jesus is the truth. His name is Jesus, because He comes to save us from self-love and its degrading consequences.

Prayer

Unto You lift I up my eyes, O You that dwells in the heavens.

Daily Word

December 13

Rejoicing

"And Mary said, My soul does magnify the Lord. And my spirit has rejoiced in God my Saviour."

> Luke 1:46, 47

Mary represents the church. The church rejoices when Jesus comes.

In relation to ourselves, Mary represents the love in our hearts that is ready to receive Jesus. His approach causes great delight, and our minds rejoice. We magnify the Lord when we fix our thoughts on Him, and see Him as the first and the last in all our concerns. We know that His coming will save us from the destroying love of ourselves. And we rejoice in God our Saviour.

Prayer

I will praise You, O Lord, among the people: and I will sing praise unto You among the nations. For Your mercy is great above the heavens: and Your truth reaches unto the clouds. Be You exalted, O God, above the heavens.

Daily Word

December 14

Taxed

"And it came to pass in those days, that there went out a decree from Caesar Augustus, that all the world should be taxed. And all went to be taxed, every one into his own city."

Luke 2:1, 3

All went to be taxed, or enrolled. We all pay taxes in one way or another. Everything we do has its own cost. There is no escape.
In those days, represents our spiritual state just before the corning of Jesus. Then, the world demands our duty of enrolment and tax paying. Soon now, things will be changed. The world will still require its due, but a higher authority will seek our enrolment in the Holy City, the New Jerusalem. A new King is approaching.

Prayer

I have longed for Your salvation, O Lord; and Your law is my delight.

December 15

From Galilee

"And Joseph also went up from Galilee, out of the city of Nazareth to be taxed with Mary, his espoused wife, being great with child."

Luke 2:4, 5

From Galilee to Judaea. In the circumstances it must have been a trying journey.

Spiritually speaking, we take this journey when we move our thoughts and affections from the things of the world to those of heaven. Our hearts then, are full of a desire for Jesus. We long for His coming. At first we proceed from a feeling of duty, but soon duty is forgotten, for Jesus comes, and all now is love. Mary represents the love in our minds that receives Jesus.

Prayer

O Lord, my soul waits for You, and in Your word do I hope. My soul waits for You more than they that watch for the morning.

Daily Word

December 16

No room

"And she brought forth her first born son, and wrapped him in swaddling clothes, and laid him in a manger: because there was no room for them in the inn."

Luke 2:7

The loveliest story in all history. In relation to ourselves it pictures the beginning of our new birth.

The swaddling clothes represent the innocence which is wrapped about the Jesus principle in our hearts. And the manger where the babe is laid, is a picture of our poor understanding which is the feeding place of the love that comes to save us.

There being no room at the inn, represents our merely natural life, that has no accommodation for the Lord.

Prayer

With You, O Lord, is the fountain of life, in Your light shall we see light. O continue Your loving kindness unto them that know You.

Daily Word

December 17

Shepherds

"And there were in the same country shepherds abiding in the field, keeping watch over their flock by night."

Luke 2:8

The same country! The shepherds and their flock. That part of your mind into which Jesus comes, is the same place where the shepherds and sheep were. It is the inner country of your soul that receives Jesus. The shepherds are your thoughts that care for your little flock of good affections that need Jesus.

Night represents selfishness and ignorance: but through this state of spiritual night, your shepherds watch over your sheep. Just as all this happened long ago, so it happens again in the fields of your mind.

Prayer

O Lord, bow down Your ear, O Lord, hear me: for I am poor and needy. Be merciful unto me, O Lord: for I cry unto You daily.

Daily Word

December 18

Glory of the Lord

"And behold, the angel of the Lord came upon them, and the glory of the Lord shone around about them: and they were sore afraid."

Luke 2:9

Long ago the angel of the Lord came to the shepherds at Bethlehem. Today, in much the same manner the angel comes to you and me: but spiritually in our minds, not naturally and outside of us.

The angel represents truth from the Lord bringing us the news of His approach. The glory of the Lord round about them pictures the wonder of His illuminating love that fills our minds. And, by being deeply afraid, is represented holy fear as we become conscious of the Lord's presence.

Prayer

O Lord, send out Your light and Your truth: let them bring me to Your holy hill, and to Your tabernacles.

Daily Word

December 19

Good Tidings

"And the angel said to them, Fear not: for behold I bring you good tidings of great joy, which shall be to all people."

Luke 2:10

Good tidings of great joy!
This is the message of Christmas. The tidings came to the shepherds through the angel. Spiritually they come to you through the message of truth from the Lord. Truth that lights the mind and which once accepted takes away all fear. Spiritually, this truth of His coming is for you, and all people.

The tidings are good, because they are the tidings of love, the love of our universal Father Who comes among us in human form to save us.

Prayer

O Lord, you are my hiding place; you shall preserve me from trouble; you shall compass me about with songs of deliverance.

Daily Word

December 20

A Saviour

"For unto you is born this day in the city of David a Saviour, which is Christ the Lord."

Luke 2:11

This day! A day about two thousand years ago. But a day of wonder, representing an eternal day. The day or state of life into which the Saviour, the truth of Divine love, is born.

The city of David is spiritually the place in your mind where the Lord's truth receives His love. It is thus that Jesus comes to you, into conditions that are able to accept Him. He cannot come unless you accept Him. There may be very little truth in your mind, but if there is enough to make a manger, He will come.

Prayer

O Lord, restore unto me the joy of Your salvation; and uphold me with Your free spirit.

Daily Word

December 21

The Sign

"And this shall be a sign to you; ye shall find the babe wrapped in swaddling clothes, lying in a manger."

Luke 2:12

The sign the angel gave the shepherd was threefold, and simple for them to understand. A babe, swaddling clothes and a manger.

The same sign is given to us today. Only it is to be found in our minds. Bethlehem is the spiritual principle within us. The babe is the beginning of the nevi love for Jesus, born in our hearts. The swaddling clothes are the innocent and lovely things from our childhood and memory, that are wrapped about and around the knowledge of Jesus. And the manger is the place where He is fed: it is our understanding.

Prayer

O Lord, let all those that seek You rejoice and be glad in You.

Daily Word

December 22

Glory to God

"And suddenly there was with the angel a multitude of the heavenly host praising God, and saying, Glory to God in the highest, and on earth peace, good will toward men."

Luke 2:13, 14

When Jesus came to our sad world, there was rejoicing among the angels. And the shepherds were partakers of it.

It is even so with us. The knowledge that Jesus has found entrance to our hearts rejoices the angels. A multitude of happy feelings spring up to say their Glory, Glory. From this joy within there comes a great peace, and we feel good will to all around us. All our feelings and thoughts cry out. Glory to God in the highest.

Prayer

O Lord, You are my goodness, and my fortress; my high tower, and my deliverer; my shield, and He in Whom I trust.

Daily Word

December 23

To Bethlehem

"And it came to pass, as the angels were gone away from them into heaven, the shepherds said one to another, Let us now go even to Bethlehem, and see this thing which is come to pass, which the Lord has made known to us."

Luke 2:15

The shepherds had seen the angels, and heard their gladness: they could never forget that experience. So with us, when once we have been conscious of the angels' presence, everything afterwards is different. Our quest in future must be Bethlehem, to learn more of what is happening in the spiritual place of the life within us. A new thing has come to pass, which the Lord is making known to us. Jesus has come.

Prayer

Lord, I cry unto You: make haste unto me; give ear unto my voice, when I cry unto You.

Daily Word

December 24

With haste

"And they came with haste, and found Mary, and Joseph, and the babe lying in a manger."

Luke 2:16

The shepherds were intensely interested in what the angel had told them. This caused them to hurry to Bethlehem.

But spiritually, haste means ardent desire; not hurrying against the clock of the natural world. When, in our hearts, we are eager to be in the presence of Jesus, our love draws us near to Him. Then like the shepherds, we find Mary and Joseph, for they represent the place within our religious life where Jesus comes. The babe lying in the manger, represents the new Jesus principle arising in our understanding.

Prayer

O come, let us sing to the Lord: let us make a joyful noise to the rock of our salvation. Let us come before Your presence, O Lord, with thanksgiving.

Daily Word

December 25

Telling the tidings

"And when they had seen it, they made known abroad the saying which was told them concerning this child."

Luke 2:17

Christmas! Its chief joy is to make known the story of Jesus.

The shepherds were the first to do this, and in this respect they were the first preachers. And He Whom the shepherds were making known, was the Good Shepherd Himself, coming among His people to seek and save lost sheep.

In relation to ourselves, when we see the coming of Jesus in our hearts, we make known abroad our love for Him, by a life that is ever changing. Changing from love of ourselves, to the love of God, and good will to all.

Prayer

Show us Your mercy, O Lord, and grant us Your salvation. Mercy and truth are met together: righteousness and peace have kissed each other.

Daily Word

December 26

The return

"And the shepherds returned, glorifying and praising God for all the things that they had heard and seen, as it was told to them."

Luke 2:20

The shepherds went to Bethlehem full of wonder. They returned glorifying and praising God.

The shepherds represent in us, those principles that care for what is good and true. Having found their way to the presence of Jesus their wonder is filled with joy. They have now heard and seen, just as the angel of truth from heaven had told them. They must now return to their ordinary duties, but they do so with new loving and thinking. Glorifying and praising God, for all the things made known to them.

Prayer

God be merciful to us; and cause His face to shine upon us; that Your way may be known upon the earth.

Daily Word

December 27

The child grew

"And the child grew, and became strong in spirit, filled with wisdom; and the grace of God was upon him.

Luke 2:40

As Jesus grew in the world outside us, so must we seek His developing presence in the world within us.

At first there is very little room, even as at Bethlehem there was no room in the inn. But now He has come to us, and we are giving him more accommodation. As we do so, He becomes stronger in our minds. His spirit of truth strengthens us, and His wisdom enlarges and blesses our understandings. Soon we are loving and thinking differently; His gracious presence enlarges our hearts and rests on all we do.

Prayer

Lord, I will not give sleep to my eyes, until I find out a place for You, a habitation for the Lord my Saviour.

Daily Word

December 28

With the teachers

"And it came to pass, that after three days they found him in the temple, sitting in the midst of the teachers, both hearing them and asking them questions."

Luke 2:46

In the temple! In relation to ourselves the temple represents the place in our minds where we worship the Lord. The teachers represent our chief thoughts and knowledge of Him.

Jesus being in the midst, hearing and asking questions, means that He is central in our spiritual seeking and questioning. Its being said to have happened after three days means after a complete period of preparation; our minds cannot properly accept the Lord except through an orderly sequence of events.

Prayer

O Lord, so teach us to number our days, that we may apply our hearts to wisdom. O satisfy us early with Your mercy.

Daily Word

December 29

Astonished

"And all that heard him were astonished at his understanding and answers."

Luke 2:47

All were astonished!
This is one of the passages of the Word that the reader can prove in his, or her, own life. Once the Lord Jesus is the centre of your questioning mind, all that is within you will be astonished. Try it yourself. Take your questions to the Lord, in His Word. Listen to His answers.

When Jesus finished talking to the people in what we call, The sermon on the mount, we read, "They were astonished at his doctrine." Astonished! That is the right word. If you seriously listen to Him yourself, you will know.

Prayer

O Lord, let Your beauty be upon us, and establish You the work of our hands upon us; yea the work of our hands establish You it.

Daily Word

December 30

Nazareth

"And He (Jesus) went down with them, and came to Nazareth, and was subject to them: but his mother kept all these sayings in her heart."

Luke 2:51

Jesus in Nazareth.

Spiritually understood, to "go down" is meant to move from an inner, or higher, state to a lower one. Nazareth in Galilee represents our outer or natural life. In relation to ourselves it pictures Jesus leaving the temple, or spiritual side of our life, to be with us in our natural daily activities. Here, He subjects Himself to the stress and strain we all experience, and shares with us all life's difficulties. By Mary "keeping His sayings in her heart," is represented our inner love for Him, which constantly cherishes His words.

Prayer

Let Your mercies come also to me, O Lord, even Your salvation, according to Your word.

Daily Word

December 31

Increase

"And Jesus increased in wisdom and stature, and in favour with God and man."

Luke 2:52

Wisdom and stature! Naturally understood it is a picture of Jesus growing by stages into manhood, as all His children do.

But spiritually understood it is a picture of our own development in wisdom and stature. As we accept Jesus and live from Him our understandings are enlightened and our love for Him is deepened. Thus we give Him more room in our lives, and He draws nearer to us.

It appears that He is increasing actually it is we, who in consequence of His nearer approach are increasing in spiritual growth. So we gain favour by loving God, and from Him one another.

Prayer

O God, You are my God, early will I seek You: my soul thirsts for You.

Daily Word

"And He opened their understanding, that they might comprehend the Scriptures."

Luke 24:45

Daily Word

Allegory: What the bible tells us

Without discarding the significance of congruent literal text – the Divine teachings within sacred scriptures - apply primarily and directly to the realm of our mind - individually and personally.

Let us have a look at what the bible itself tells us:

"Open my eyes, that I may see wondrous things from Your law. I am a stranger in the earth, do not hide Your commandments from me."

Psalm 119:18,19

"..the words are closed up and sealed till the time of the end. ...none of the wicked shall understand, but the wise shall understand."

Daniel 12:9,10

"They shall run to and fro, seeking the word of the Lord, but shall not find it."

Amos 8:12

"He who has ears, let him hear! ....it has been given to you to know the mysteries of

Daily Word

the kingdom of heaven, but to them is has not been given... Therefore I speak to them in parables, because seeing they do not see, and hearing they do not hear, nor do they understand."

> Matthew 13:9,11,13

"And beginning at Moses and all the Prophets, He expounded to them in all the Scriptures the things concerning Himself. .. And they said to one another, 'Did not our heart burn within us while He talked with us on the road, and while He opened the Scriptures to us?'"

> Luke 24:27,32

"I still have many things to say to you, but you cannot bear them now. However, when He, the Spirit of truth, has come, He will guide you into all truth."

> John 16:12-13

"These things I have spoken to you in figurative language.."

> John 16:25

"..the letter kills, but the Spirit gives life."

> 2 Corinthians 3:6

Daily Word

"Tell me, you who desire to be under the law, do you not hear the law? ..which things are symbolic.."

                                    Galatians 4:21,24

"..praying also for us, that God would open to us a door for the word, to speak the mystery of Christ.."

                                    Colossians 4:3

"..the way into the Holiest of All was not yet made manifest while the first tabernacle was still standing. It was symbolic.."

                                    Hebrews 9:8

"Give ear, O my people, to my law; Incline your ears to the words of my mouth. I will open my mouth in a parable; I will utter dark sayings of old."

                                    Psalm 78:1,2

"But even to this day, when Moses is read, a veil lies on their heart. Nevertheless when one turns to the Lord, the veil is taken away. Now the Lord is the Spirit; and where the Spirit of the Lord is, there is liberty."

                                    2 Corinthians 3:15-17

This hidden treasure map to personal spiritual application can be found through the understanding of ancient symbolism if coupled with a sincere willingness to be led by truth from the Word on a quest to develop our true inner character.

> *"Read the Word, and believe in the Lord, and you will see the truths which should constitute your faith and life; for all in the Christian world draw their doctrine from the Word as from the only fountain. ... every man whose soul desires it is capable of seeing the truths of the Word in the light..., provided indeed he hungers after it, and seeks it from the Lord"*
>
> Emanuel Swedenborg, Apocalypse Revealed 224

There are three fundamental assumptions to be understood which underpin Freedom Philosophy's approach to any scripture study:

1: The Divine is the source of all wisdom, all love and therefore all truth and life.

Daily Word

This is not limited to the physical and literal text of the books in the bible. We can access and connect with the great I Am through opening our inner self, yearning to learn the truth and by seeking to serve others meaningfully. There are even many other great sacred texts that channel The Word and through which the Divine, Jehovah God, can teach and transform us.

> *"From His omnipotence God created the universe, and introduced order into each thing and all things in it ... God also preserves the universe, and unceasingly watches over the order of it with its laws; and when anything falls from order He brings it back and makes it whole again."*
>
> Emanuel Swedenborg, True Christian Religion 74

2: Our mind is not physical and already operates in the spiritual realm.

Some call it dream world, world of spirits or the metaphysical realm. It doesn't matter what you call it, the truth is our thoughts and feelings originate from it and remain non-physical. We already connect with heaven right now, by curing a heavenly state of being within ourselves. Our ability to be transformed comes courtesy of the all-knowing source of all, through divine principles operating since the beginning of time.

> *"Everything that is done according to Divine order is inwardly open to the Lord, and thus has heaven in it. Divine order is for the Lord to flow in through the interiors of man into his exteriors, thus through the will of man into his action. .. How a man must live for it to be according to order, the Word teaches..."*
>
> Emanuel Swedenborg, Arcana Coelestia 8513

3: The natural world and our experience within it, does not operate independently from our mind and the Divine, but in essence reflects the Divine through us.

Because of this, our outer experience depends on our connection with God and can be traced back to those divine principles operative within the human mind.

> *"Whatever in universal nature has not correspondence with the spiritual world cannot exist, having no cause from which to exist, consequently from which to subsist. The things that are in nature are nothing but effects; their causes are in the spiritual world... Nor can the effect subsist unless the cause is constantly in it, because the effect ceases when the cause ceases. Regarded in itself the effect is nothing else than the cause, but so clothed outwardly as to enable the cause to act as a cause in a lower sphere. ...*
> *Hence it is also plain that as each and all things in the world have come forth from the Divine, they continue to come forth from the Divine."*
>
> Emanuel Swedenborg, Arcana Coelestia 5711

The closer you look, the more everything is in harmony and a perfect representation of us. The symbolism within the Bible (and other sacred texts), ties perfectly back to the operation of the human mind and its associated states and qualities. This is where we find the understanding of the symbolism.

> *"All things in The Word both in general and in particular, ... down to the most minute iota, signify and enfold within them spiritual and heavenly things.. that the Word is really of this character might be known from the single consideration that being the Lord's and from the Lord it must of necessity contain within it such things as belong to heaven ... and that unless it did so it could not be called the Lord's Word, nor could it be said to have any life in it. .....the Lord, who is the very Life itself."*
>
> Emanuel Swedenborg, Arcana Coelestia 2

I believe the symbolism that is being partially revealed in this book was well understood in ancient times, but has since long been forgotten. We can trace remnants of it back within the oldest known languages, within myths, stories and even those sayings that have survived in the modern world. You only need to bring a humble state of mind: a willingness to be led by the Lord.

Daily Word

"Speak what is high! high! Let what is ancient come out of your mouth"

> 1 Samuel 2:3

"I will utter dark sayings of old"

> Psalms 78:2

I promise, that once you start studying The Word with these ancient keys through allegory and symbolism, your scriptural understanding will open your inner world and your spiritual life will be transformed and never be the same again.

Cor

3 ways to read the Bible

You might be surprised that there are more than one way to read anything, let alone the sacred scriptures. I believe there is a traditional, a practical and a spiritual way to read the scriptures. Let me here briefly outline the three distinctly different ways of reading the scriptures as I see it.

Traditionally

One may also call this the literal or natural method. This method is aimed at the literal text alone and is useful for memorising stories, finding references and learning historical context. It is a way to enjoy the prose and beauty of the language upon which much of Shakespeare is based too. This method helps us predominantly builds up stories for recalling at a later time from our memory.

It particularly applies when reading the scriptures cover-to-cover, such as daily bible reading programs or presenting bible stories to children. The same applies when we listen to audio bibles or when we watch a video based on biblical stories. It is no different to the way we read any novel for entertainment or seek to gain any knowledge for the sake of knowing.

Here is a bible verse many will know from having memorised it.
> *"If anyone thirsts, let him come to Me and drink. He who believes in Me, as the Scripture has said, out of his heart will flow rivers of living water."*
>
> The Word, John 7:37-38

I think, well I hope, you can agree with me that reading scripture in this way has a place, but presents a very limited path. It puts all the responsibility on the text to present itself and this method offers no deeper approach than mere memory knowledge.

Practically

The practical method is not directly aimed at the literal text alone, but focuses on personal guidance for life application. It seeks to find rules to follow or examples of life application and may therefore also be called the application method. It applies when we infer character qualities from biblical figures, draw on proverbs, laws and sayings on how to live and follow direct examples or rules taught in various places. Looking for practical support in the sacred scriptures sees an extra layer of meaning and effect coming from the various biblical stories.

You can see there is a personal level of interpretation required with how to give effect to the practical advice derived from the literal text in sacred scripture. This is possibly too the level at which most misunderstanding and conflict occurs as a result of doctrinal application differences.

Here is a bible verse we refer to as the Golden rule. This same law is found in every religion in one form or another.

> *"In everything, therefore, treat people the same way you want them to treat you, for this is the Law and the Prophets."*
>
> The Word, Matthew 7:12

Perhaps you can see somewhat of a

progression?

As we look to practical application, the actual literal text becomes a little less important beyond the guidance it offers informing the interpretation. This must by necessity be so, because not all text is absolute and without any ambiguity. Reason being is that language is contextual and dependent on cultural norms and to lesser extent personal interpretation from experience.

Spiritually

This method is seemingly the most contentious, because it mostly disregards the meaning of the literal text, but focuses on direct personal application. It can also be referred to as the symbolic or allegorical method and with it separates the interpreted meaning from the literal meaning, it should not be considered arbitrarily.

Within this there are essentially two distinct sub-methods:

A. The allegorical interpretation in which there is a consistent level of representation (or correspondence) between the natural presentation and the spiritual meaning that underpins it. For example, it is well known (on the most rudimentary level of allegory) that by light or to see is actually meant to understand and that by taking up the cross is not meant to literally carry a heavy wooden structure, but to take responsibility for our character and behaviour and so doing what we must.

B. The personal interpretation in which we meditate and pray to understand the personal message the Word has for us. It seeks to gain insight for spiritual correction and is the only method by which we have a direct connection with the Lord.

Only these two related ways of approaching the sacred scripture spiritually carry the mechanism by which The Lord is actually acknowledged as the Living Word. In other words, where the Word is allowed to live.

The following verse offers a great example of where the bible itself gives us insight into it's living spiritual nature.

> *"And beginning at Moses and all the Prophets, He expounded to them in all the*

Daily Word

*Scriptures the things concerning Himself. ..
And they said to one another, 'Did not our
heart burn within us while He talked with
us on the road, and while He opened the
Scriptures to us?"*

The Word, Luke 24:27,32

I wholeheartedly recommend studying the allegorical nature of the sacred scriptures, as well as take time to regularly meditate and allow The Word through the scriptures offer you guidance in this way.

Final Note

Before leaving you with the idea that these methods of approaching the way you read the sacred scriptures are exclusive, as well as distinct, allow me to make it clear to you that, while the deeper allegorical meaning may be totally removed from what presents on the surface level and therefore seemingly unconnected, in the ideal circumstance it will be true on all levels at the same time. However we must constantly bear in mind that the Lord (The Word) is in fact only considered with our spiritual character - our heart and not so much with what we do or know.

This is also how you will find the distinction between biblical text useful for teaching and those parts that I believe can actually be considered the Word. The Word, which is infinite and complete, must be consistent and true on the spiritual level first and foremost: the cause of our reality. If you look for it, you will find a consistent correspondence between the natural and the spiritual. This is the Law of Correspondence and magical once you get to understand it.

You can study the allegories in sacred scripture or try sacred meditation on scriptures in the Freedom Philosophy community.

Original Title:
Daily Readings from The Word with Commentary and Prayers by Reg Lang
by:
Missionary Society of the New Church London

Now edited by Cornelis PJ Visser-Marchant
published by: Freedom Philosophy

This edited version was prepared as a tribute to the original work (1962) by Reg Lang, which is now no longer available in print.

Drawing from the Bible and revelations of Emanuel Swedenborg, you will discover the forgotten ancient sacred wisdom that holds the key to understanding The Word and strengthen your faith in a personal connection with the Divine: our Lord Jesus Christ!

This work is therefore of considerable value (like the 'Pearl of Great Price') to everyone seeking to draw from everlasting well of truth and our Lord Jesus Christ: **The Living Word**.

Daily Word

For more information:
www.freedomphilosophy.life

"..you shall know the truth, and the truth shall make you free."

John 8:32

Freedom Philosophy promotes a meaningful spirituality, teaching the essential practices of an effective spiritual life using ancient principles. When practised, these spiritual principles help us to free our minds, grow in wisdom, discover our purpose and strengthen our faith and connection with the Divine.

Daily Word

www.ingramcontent.com/pod-product-compliance
Lightning Source LLC
Chambersburg PA
CBHW031229290426
44109CB00012B/222